WOMEN

GABRIELA MISTRAL

WOMEN

Edited by
MARJORIE AGOSÍN & JACQUELINE C. NANFITO

Translated by
JACQUELINE C. NANFITO

WHITE PINE PRESS · BUFFALO, NEW YORK

WHITE PINE PRESS
P.O. Box 236, Buffalo, New York 14201

Publication of this book was made possible, in part,
by grants from the National Endowment for the Arts
and the New York State Council on the Arts.

Cover art: "Alfonsina," by Emma Alvarez Piñeiro.
Oil, 56" x 44", 1985

Book design: Elaine LaMattina

Printed and bound in the United States of America

1 3 5 7 9 10 8 6 4 2

Library of Congress Cataloging-in-Publication Data
Mistral, Gabriela, 1889-1957.
Women / edited by Marjorie Agosín and Jacqueline C. Nanfito ;
trasnlated by Jacqueline C. Nanfito
p.   cm. — (Secret Weavers Series ; v. 15)
Includes bibliographical references.
ISBN 1-893996-09-3 (pbk. : alk. paper)
1. Women—Biography. I. Agosín, Marjorie. II. Nanfito, Jacqueline C. (Jacqueline Clare), 1957-.
III. Title. IV. Series.

HQ1123 .M53 2001

2001017660

CONTENTS

WOMEN

GABRIELA MISTRAL

MARJORIE AGOSÍN

Anomalous, eccentric, prolific, both patient and impatient, always revising her poems, eternally wandering and above all, permanently a foreigner, Gabriela Mistral, almost one hundred years after her birth, continues to awaken passions, rancor and a deep ambiguity which is oftentimes its most exquisite privilege.

Who is Gabriela Mistral really? Is she the teacher in Elqui, in the remote areas of northern of Chile,? Or is she the educational reformer who traveled, invited by the government of José Vasconcelos to reform the Mexican schools? Is Gabriela Mistral just the winner of the Nobel Prize in Literature in 1945 when, after the pain of World War II, the world's vision focused on America, the continent which was less barbaric than the Europe which grants these prizes? As time went by, Gabriela became all of these things: humble teacher, political figure, women's rights activist, delegate for her country to ratify the Human Rights Declaration and an icon of her people whose face appeared first on national stamps during the tumultuous years of the military dictatorship and later on Chilean currency.

Gabriela Mistral is a figure who perpetuates disjointed images of benevolence and arrogance, of love for the indigenous people and paternalism. She continues to be Gabriela, the ever-present voice in a Latin America struggling with the same problems that she showed to the world through her poetry, her

3

words and her political activism.

This introduction traces a poetic-historical itinerary of Gabriela Mistral's life, focusing on well-known works in order to later introduce you to texts that are, to date, hardly known: the *recados*.[1] These short pieces dedicated to praising, announcing, or denouncing events and historical characters of her era are literary jewels. Skillfully translated by Jacqueline C. Nanfito, Mistral's *recados* on women are united here for the first time.

DESOLACIÓN

Although Gabriela Mistral's life was characterized by a constant wandering through the landscape—in North America as well as in Central and South America and Europe—her anchor and her poetic presence were in her birthplace, the Elqui Valley, an area of impressive beauty, delicate hills, intense sun, delicate streams, fig and olive trees. Elqui surprises all travelers with a landscape not found anywhere else in Chile. It is also surprising to discover its mystical and biblical character. It is a region surrounded by silence and at the same time filled with the melodious sounds of the rivers and winds that surround it.

Elqui could well be a landscape from Jerusalem or from Toledo. Gabriela Mistral was raised in agricultural surroundings with a strong pastoral presence, surrounded by mountains and trees. She herself states that she could never abandon such a landscape in her work. At the same time, her poetic topography became richer and more complex as it encompassed the Americas. Gabriela's poetry describes in particular detail the Caribbean landscape, which had appeared only sporadically before in Latin American literature.[2] Notwithstanding her almost obsessive longing for Chile, Gabriela wanted to experience other cultures, to be a post-modern woman, to be transcultural and above all, hybrid. She was among the first writers to incorporate the Caribbean and Puerto Rican presence in her vision of America.

Gabriela Mistral studied to become a teacher in what was called, at the time, the Normal School, where, almost exclusively, all the teachers in Chile were taught. The teacher par excellence was a woman dedicated to fomenting the well-being of others, as Gabriela so powerfully exemplifies in her poem "The Rural Teacher":

> The poor teacher. Her realm is not human.
> Thus in the painful sowing of Israel
> she wore tan skirts and wore no jewels on her hands

and her spirit was a gigantic jewelry box!

Like an overflowing glass
was her soul
ready to empty itself on humanity
and her human life was the dilated breach
that characteristically opens up for the father to throw forth light.[3]

The tone of "La maestra rural" is typical of the poems in *Desolación*, the first book of poems published by Gabriela Mistral. It is an elegiac and religious tone, but at the same time it questions things, as we can see in the poem "Nocturno místico": "Our Father who art in Heaven/why have you forgotten me?"[4]

The critics of her time and the reviews in the provincial newspapers praised this first book, which ironically, was published in 1922 in New York City, where she would later die. The book was published under the auspices of the Spanish Institute of Columbia University and scholar Federico de Onís, who was struck by a poetry so uncluttered by adjectives. It was a poetry capable of forging alliances between the mystical and the telluric through a voice that questioned or doubted, but which also represented the forgotten beings, especially women.

Around 1914, Gabriela Mistral was known not only as a rural teacher but as winner of the Floral Games, a prestigious Latin American literary award, and author of the famous "Sonnets of Death,"[5] which were attributed to the suicide of her true love, the young Romelio Urretia. For many years, as Jaime Quezada says, these "Sonnets of Death," the poet's shyness, her solitude and the absence of any children defined Gabriela, the person, and her work. More than fifty years went by before Gabriela Mistral's true face was revealed: that of a passionate woman ready to fight for an American identity.

Desolación gave Gabriela Mistral a place in the literary world. Her book was read in universities and the image of Gabriela as a wanderer and traveler was absorbed by the people. After she won the Floral Games, she traveled throughout Chile teaching reading and writing in schools in the most remote areas: the Andes, Traiguen, Temuco and Santiago. These rural Andean towns and others, such as Punta Arenas, the southernmost city in the world, gave way to a continuous and extensive geography which was key to Gabriela's work, especially her poems, which always included the powerful elements of absence and melancholy. But Gabriela Mistral did not cease writing notes and book commentaries in the provincial newspapers, thus uniting her interior poetic world and the exterior world that updated her and gave her a place in the artistic sphere.

It was the same topics, worked with great constancy—the rural teacher, Christ's life, questions about faith, the Chilean landscape, solitary and remote—which she carried within her almost as a birthmark. In "Paisajes de la Patagonia," Gabriela says:

> The thick fog
> eternal so I will not forget where
> I have thrown myself into the sea with its briny waves
> the soil to which I arrived has no spring
> it has a long night in which my mother hides me.

That long austral night was the emblem, the metaphor of the internalized territory, the nation and the feeling of being a stranger within her own history and her own country. It is important to question why, although she participated constantly in the national history of Chile as a teacher and as a writer in the newspapers, in her conversations with and declarations to the press, she considered herself an outsider. Gabriela was and was not from Chile. She spent her whole life coming to terms with her place within the country that gave her speech yet relegated her to invisibility and very belatedly granted her the honors she deserved. It's important to remember that Gabriela won the Nobel Prize before she was awarded Chile's National Literature Prize, a somewhat unique phenomenon.

Many times I've wondered what it is in Gabriela's poetic voice that dazzles or causes rejection. The answer lies in the fact that her voice is an authentic and innovative expression, different from all the other poets of her time, especially the group of women who dominated the Latin American literature of the 1920s. By this I mean writers such as Alfonsina Storni, Juana Ibarbourou or Delmira Agustini, women whose literature is intimate, personal and courageous when researching gender issues and altering the Latin American landscape. Gabriela's poetry is tinted by symbolic cultural space. She introduces Latin American topics as a continuation of the dialogue on what it means to be from the south. She introduces the concept of women's occupations, like being a teacher, without articulating that in teaching lies the beginning of a nation's history: the liberation of women when they are educated. Gabriela understands that very early on, the secularization of education will be her most essential legacy as well as that which will offer the possibility for women to acquire a public space of power and a political voice for women.

Gabriela Mistral is capable within a poem of talking about faith and landscape, about women and history. She understands both the person who prays and the person who breaks into song. Between the word implied and the spoken word we see the emergence of a unique and vibrant Gabriela whose poetry puts us that much closer to the rhythm of the clay as well as the political gestures that speak of freedom. Gabriela embarks on a journey that oscillates between the personal and intimate and the public and collective, raising the flag of women's plight with faith and vision.

TALA: POETIC IMAGERY

If Gabriela defines herself as a constant traveler who has no home which lasts beyond her consular term, or who often changes addresses, this image of the wanderer merges with the image of the figure who never abandons the childhood landscape. No matter how often Gabriela appears to the critics as the cosmopolitan figure, we must not forget that first and foremost, she came from a rural family of little means and a poor agricultural area at a time when power was still measured by the richness of the land.

The Elqui Valley is a peasant region of Mediterranean climate where cattle wander the hills and the Aconcagua River Pass, which leads to the valley and the whole Andean area. Like the surrounding regions, the valley suffered from the arrival of the Spaniards as well as the conquest and agrarian reforms to the area. From the end of the 18th century to the mid-19th century, it was a fragmented valley, divided by landlords who split the valley up into various small neglected tracts of landed real estate. Gabriela's family was one of the small land owners of the area, but Gabriela's education was essentially rural.

It is important to note how Gabriela was brought up and how this tinged her vision of the world. Molded by nature and the people who surrounded her, the natural world—valleys, mountains and river—is a strong presence in her work. She does not choose for her poetry the world of witches and magic or the region's folklore. Her cosmic vision is rooted in the oral history so typical of the Old Testament, which later dominated her life and made her one of the few Latin American writers who dedicated her poems to the Jewish people and to certain women of the Bible, such as Ruth.

During the time that Gabriela was growing up, readings from the Bible were generally those from the New Testament. Scholars believe that her family must have found phrases and writings that dated back to a Bible of the Old

Testament, possibly brought to Chile by Protestant shepherds at the turn of the century. The readings Gabriela quotes come from the Bible of creation and origin. Her poetry, and her other literary work, as far as one can tell, do not contain the enchanted and mystical creatures that are common to the Elqui region folklore, nor does she seem to refer to an anima cult. However, almost twenty years after *Tala*, Gabriela Mistral revealed the secrets of death and the nocturnal journeys of the dead in her extensive and perplexing "Poema de Chile," published posthumously, where a dead woman returns to visit her America.

After various posts as a rural teacher in Chile, Gabriela began her life as a wanderer in Mexico. If Mexico represented for Gabriela the great journeys through America, it also reinforced her feelings of being a foreigner both outside and within her country. Accused of being an "outsider" who was going to resolve the educational reform issues, Gabriela decided to abruptly end her stay in Mexico and published those writings for women on which she had been working for years. These writings, which to a modern-day reader may appear superfluous, gained great importance for many generations because they created a canon of voices with the sole purpose of educating women.

Gabriela wrote an apologetic introduction which at times reminds us of a treatise on the weak, as Josefina Ludmer would say.[6] When referring to Sor Juana Inés de la Cruz, Gabriela says that they both wrote letters from a foreigner's perspective and for a foreigner's perspective. Little has been said about the tone of those letters, but I gather that this Mexican experience made her feel forever an outsider and filled her subsequent work with the stories of hiding and masks that would become part of her poetic legacy and her contradictory personality, tinged with some rancor.

The critics of Mistral's work, which until a decade ago were predominantly men who emphasized those aspects of Mistral's work which defined her as the mother/teacher archetype, describe *Tala* as the most serene book she wrote due to the Americanist outline of the poems. I think that all of Mistral's texts maintained a feeling of Americanism, including the section of *Desolación* where she presents the idea of a Patagonian landscape and the area around Magallanes which almost fifty years later gains extraordinary importance. *Tala* proposes a transcultural vision of America and its people. That is to say, it is a text where the voices of silence become part of the landscape, where the legacy of Americanism joins the legacy of an American vision. Clay pots, rivers and nature join voices with Gabriela, the poet who discovers landscapes and the poetry that delineates them.

The hymns dedicated to the "Tropical Sun" or the "Praises for the Island of Puerto Rico" represent one of the peak achievements of her poetic genius, but they are also the beginnings of a lyric that is not epic nor grandiloquent, but rather analytical of the materials, the bread, the wheat and the ashes. In *Tala*, geography describes an overwhelming nature which is profoundly human and earthly. If in *Desolación* and other dispersed poems there is a saintly and religious Gabriela, here we see a wandering Gabriela who dares to look up at the sky, but this time it is not God who assumes the role of the protagonist. Nor is he the object of her questions. Gabriela Mistral portrays herself, and the images she sees reflected are those of a stranger, a wanderer and a woman without a face. *Tala* is significant as a book not only because of its unifying vision of America, but also because of the direction and courage of its questions.

One of the most powerful and enlightening articles about *Tala*, written by Adriana Valdés,[7] proposes a new vision of Gabriela and her poetry. She does not deny the importance of the Indo-American spirit, but her point is that in *Tala* Gabriela assumes another voice which lives within her: the voice of the foreigner, the old voice: Sibyl's voice. It is evident in the section entitled "The crazy women" that Gabriela outlines a new way of being a woman which goes hand in hand with the occult, the secret and maybe the magical aspect of things. Much has been said about Gabriela the teacher, the educational reformer, and the consul, but very little has been said of Gabriela the Sybil or the Cassandra. Adriana Valdés tells us that in *Tala* Mistral offers us the possibility of speaking out as a transgressor. She is not the woman looking for God. She is the mother and she is searching for herself.

Tala is a book where women's identity takes on varying proportions. *Tala* is also a book of great transgressions and this sense of not belonging to the established canons of the world will mark a great portion of Gabriela's poetry. For example, in "Nocturno de la consumación" we see the presence of the dead Christ and this image occupies the "place of the mother," thus granting itself the luxury and possibility of speaking out. Here Mistral approaches a crucial territory, that of language, in both its poetic function and its historical function for women, and it forgets women's roles as minor subjects who only receive God's sacrament. In *Tala* we have the invocation to a dead mother:

Mother of mine in sleep
I wander the thistle-filled landscapes
a black mountain which we must circle

9

always to reach the other mountain
and you are on top of the next one, vaguely
but always there is another golden mountain
which must be circled to give way
to the mountain of your joy and mine.[8]

The subject of this poem is the mother and it is Gabriela who calls her in
the voice of the one who searches. In *Tala* there are memorable poems filled
with polished lyricism and the unencumbered rhythm of words, but even
more so, they are filled by a sense of desolation which accompanies the
rhythm of the lives of so many women alien to their own lives and histories:

She speaks with a local accent
of her barbarian seas
I don't know what algae or what sands.
She prays to God without a load or weight
aging as if she were dying
in our orchard which made us strangers.

And how could we forget the memorable verses about old age:

You forgot the unforgettable death
like a landscape, like a job,
a tongue
and death also forgot its face
because it forgets faces with eyebrows.

If there is an obsession for America, there is also a desire to name her and
to recognize amd make intimate in the faces without a name the moments in
which women assume silence as the power of old age.

Gabriela explores a great portion of the themes of her literary work published in *Tala* and in "Poema de Chile," which is a meditation and exploration
of the American continent from an ecological point of view. *Tala* liberates
Gabriela and enables her to speak about women, her powers and hidden
strengths, such as the mystery of creativity. All of Gabriela's approaches to
women's spaces are based on a perspective of education or human rights and
children's rights. In *Tala*, Gabriela speaks of the privilege of insanity as a possibility to achieve freedom and she dedicates a series of poems to insane

women where she insinuates that insanity is the power of the marginal and, obviously, of women.

Tala, as Adriana Valdés points out, is a book of encounters and intersections. It is a literary vision that mobilizes from the small, almost claustrophobic, space of the valley, to place Gabriela as a woman with her lyric and herself. *Tala* is an essential book that marks the path of Latin American lyricism since it was published at the same time as Vicente Huidobro's *Altazor*, a surreal epic poem, and Pablo Neruda's *Residencias* I and II. *Tala* is different from these other texts since the spaces created by Huidobro and Neruda are spaces where one discovers the vertiginous experiences of the First and Second World Wars, the tenebrous fall of surrealism and the ambiguity of identity. *Tala* is a book that speaks about women's hidden powers, the divine and often lacerated power. *Tala* has images of priestesses, of the power within the self, of strangers assuming power within a land that belongs to no one and, possibly, within their own lands.

LAGAR: WOMEN'S TERRITORY

Up to a certain point, *Lagar* is an elaboration of the themes found in *Tala* but it is a book that inserts itself more solidly in world politics and European history, as we will see in the poems dedicated to war and prisoners. Here, Gabriela is perhaps less hermetic and less of a transgressor, but still, she assumes the voice of the clairvoyant poet and the role that she must take to denounce history. *Lagar* is then the sum of all the worries and preoccupations in her literary work, her profound humanism and compassion, her conscience and peace. It is in this field that Gabriela was of vital importance and we must rescue the significance of her role in the various manifestations in favor of peace, as well as her vital participation in the signing of the Declaration of Human Rights as Chile's delegate.

Lagar, written almost at the end of her life, is dedicated to assuming the voice of the clairvoyant woman who retells the horrors and at the same time tries to rebuild a more just society. We must remember that historically, Mistral assumes a very clear position when she speaks out against fascism in Spain during the time when she was Chile's consul and also during her time in Brazil, of which little is known.

Gabriela wrote *Lagar* during her last consular stay in Brazil, and this is a time close to her death and to the death of her beloved nephew. It is a time of personal and historical reflection, and this book would be the only one of the four she wrote to be originally published in Chile. This lack of interest by

Chilean publishers indicated an absolute indifference to her work while she was alive. Before her death, Gabriela returned for a very brief period to Chile and she traveled throughout the country. She was the foreign poet, the visitor who always felt part of the country of absence or of the country she invoked.

Lagar, as Jaime Quezada points out in his introduction to La prosa y poesia de Gabriela Mistral in an important Venezuelan edition, is the end of a poetic cycle begun with Desolación. I would say that Lagar is a more universal book. It is a book in which empathy and human suffering are fully shared in a text that shows solidarity and fraternity, as we see in the poem entitled "La guerra" ("The War"). The poet also inserts herself as part of the interior war that she had to live:

> Come brother tonight
> to pray with your sister who has
> neither children, nor mother, nor a present caste.

Lagar assumes Gabriela's and the planet's orphanage and loneliness, but it also evokes the solitude of man when faced with destruction. If Tala represents a fertile, beautiful and daring book, Lagar is the conscience of the realm, of the earth surrounded by fog and ashes, of that which disappears and only remains through the power to evoke.

> Traces of what is not
> the fugitive man
> I only have the traces
> and the weight of his body
> and the wind which carries him
> neither signals nor a name
> neither the country nor the town.

Devoid of a human and a national cultural geography to recover and rename, Gabriela silently and during her residence in the United States, almost at the end of her life, began "Poema de Chile," a new poetic experience through the voice of a woman, shrouded but alive, who possesses the ease of naming and telling. She is a dead woman who travels the vast Chilean and Latin American territory and she names what she sees: fauna, forests, and the color of the sky. It is a book that soars and one flies through its pages, accompanying a ghostly woman often called insane by the other characters in the poem as a gesture of power and tenderness. It is precisely this insanity which allows her to learn about the geography that she so loved from an ecological point of view where the earthly is neither a political nor historical space. All borders are erased as well as the spaces between life and death.

The insanity described in "Poema de Chile" is a wise madness that plays with the image of a dead woman who frees herself and lives after death. In contrast, the insane women in *Tala* appear mainly as disturbed, delirious and desperate women made insane by their loneliness. It is also interesting to note the way in which "Poema de Chile" is constructed. Through this poem, Gabriela continues to ally herself with a sense of permanence in the arts, with memory and the denial of oblivion.

There are similarities between *Poema de Chile* and the poems in *Ternura*. The latter anthology, seldom discussed by the critics and considered by many as a minor work, attempts to interweave the life experiences and the games of children in America, to celebrate animated objects and introduce a woman who narrates stories, a globetrotter, a woman who represents the face of Gabriela and also participates in a fabulous and creative childhood. *Poema de Chile* recovers the astonishment and the enthusiasm we once felt for nature, for the leaves of certain tress, the names of certain birds. More than a praise for Chile's nature, it is an offering of love to those small and invisible things in a vast and mysterious geography. *Poema de Chile* is a glance from the perspective of a dead woman at the paths of life and the nature that explores alternate worlds. Gabriela, already letting go of her earthly surroundings, is capable of sharpening the senses and creating again what she had begun in *Lagar* and *Tala*: a transnational and transcultural vision of history and of the American culture. Gabriela also continues to be well ahead of her time, not only in terms of the ecological recovery of certain elements in our living nature, but in her descriptive verses. In *Poema de Chile* Gabriela begins to forge a strong relationship with history—not the history of facts and wars, but that which Miguel de Unamuno would call "the intrahistory of history," which is daily life and has the face and the presence of a woman. Then, in this poem, Gabriela continues with this clear portrait of the peasants' and indigenous children's lives in Atacama. Gabriela is one more voice, a narrator of innumerable deeds and histories and of tiny things, which reminds us of Neruda, who later wrote about the greatness of the human realm through the presence of small yet majestic objects such as tomatoes, fried conch, books and socks.

Unlike her other books—with the exception of *Ternura* where there is love for all small things and a sensual dedication to the history of animals—*Poema de Chile* and the shrouded poet, traveling light, create a vibrant and profoundly human dialogue through her guide, an indigenous child from Atacama who travels and discovers with her human and natural geography. These discoveries turn geography into a lyrical history of the spoken word and the people's customs, dating back to numerous of Gabriela's writings which were only *recados*, brief messages which took on the presence of an oral tradition in her poetry as a new way to create a personal and collective memory. Maybe this is the reason why the mystery found in storytelling, whether by children or adults, is what best describes Mistral's short stories, brief anecdotes, prose poems and, most particularly, her *recados*.

THE RECADOS

The *recados*, short messages, letters and literary essays, were part of Gabriela's literary work for more than thirty-five years. She obstinately sent them to newspapers in America, and especially to the well-known Costa Rican paper *Repertorio Americano*. Dispersed over so many years, as time went on they were relegated to oblivion. Our greatest wish was to collect some of those *recados* which talk about women and present them to the English speaking audience. This collection of *recados* about women will without doubt allow us to know and analyze Gabriela Mistral, her relationship with her culture and her identity, and the power of her imagery.

It is interesting to ask what these *recados* imply and what part they occupy within Gabriela's creative repertoire. The *recados* reveal a tenacity and constancy to belong in the world and evoke events that surrounded Gabriela Mistral and her history. An analysis of these *recados* will allow us to get closer to the preoccupations of the historical time in which Gabriela lived. Very little has been said about Gabriela's vast library—although she moved often, Gabriela had a very large library—or about her curiosity in the most varied themes ranging from botany to zoology, as she traveled through pre-Columbian and contemporary history.

Gabriela's *recados* were published in the Costa Rican *Repertorio Americano* and were compiled for the first time by distinguished professor Mario Céspedes and published in 1971 with a brief second edition in 1978 in Chile. It must be noted that the *recados* have not been studied in detail. They are almost unknown and they reveal great clues about Gabriela's personality. For example, they show us her thoughts about what literary critics said about her works ("Letter to My Biographer"), her love for Chile, science and women of science ("Recado to Madame Curie"). The *recados* we present here evoke a great passion for women. Jaime Quezada states that few writers since have rendered women's presence and wisdom as so important or shown such an appreciation for women, both Chilean and foreign.

Mistral cared very little for the limitations imposed by nationality and race. To define women, Mistral uses a word that is very much her own and which will accompany her throughout history. She calls it *mujerío*.[9] This unique word was always very close to her preoccupations, in the prologue to the book or the public conference, in her letters or at the table where she shared maize and milk. The woman of Mistral's era, whether teacher, artist, writer or simply housewife, would be an enthusiastic and revitalizing motivation for the writer.

Without the strident and unfriendly voices of personas, Gabriela's art is of that effervescent period when women were demanding the right to vote and a strong female presence in the assemblies. Gabriela herself states that "Women gather only to rub elbows with the politicians and achieve suffrage or to organize charitable activities." This feminism points to a struggle for social action, educational reforms and peace. It was a struggle in which she participated until the end of her days and she did it not only as an effort to vindicate human rights and to make women's rights part of human rights. In this area, she was a pioneer and a visionary.

The *recados*, by definition, are brief essays, two to three pages long. Sometimes they are written as letters, and Gabriela calls them elegies. Each one of them has the presence of the oral element—the possibility of reading them to an accessible audience—they belong to that hybrid and complex zone between literary criticism and subjective impressions. What is most fascinating about these *recados* is the fact that they reveal the quality of what is immediate, like a history that tells something that must be shared. The *recados* do not have an ultimate goal of presenting the objective reality of these facts, but rather, they wish to show us and allow us to feel how that reality had an impact on Gabriela Mistral's life. That is to say, they are brief meditations, glimpses where the personal becomes the historical, where the writer's place finds its way into the social configuration of its time.

María Ester Martínez is one of the few scholars who dedicated an essay to Mistral's work as a creator of *recados*, linking this experience with that of a literary critic. It is an experience that can be associated with the common reader, so-called in the brief articles and review written by Virginia Woolf. Martínez believes that these *recados* are valuable not only as historical documents, but also as a key part of literary criticism. She states:

> The texts in which Gabriela expresses her critical review of
> various authors and works are called *recados*. We could add
> the literary adjective since in these texts, aside from fulfilling
> the goal in spirit that Mistral gave to the *recado*, to be a text
> whose purpose it is to inform, value and express an opinion,
> she gives an opinion that allows us to know and value the
> knowledge and reception that foreign and national literary
> works had.

Martínez defines a *recado* using the definition of the Spanish Royal Academy
and Mistral stays within this definition. *Recado* is also defined as a message
that reveals a memory, and the last definition in the dictionary is to give a gift.
With this in mind, Mistral exerts a novel and important action, that of giving
praise, through words, to certain beloved books, such as her *recado* dedicated
to Rilke's works or the one filled with love and fervor entitled "San
Francisco's motives." Gabriela's *recados* are a gift, the gift of memory and the
experience that is implied in writing from one's memories. This can explain
the deep devotion and loyalty Gabriela felt for nurturing her personal correspondence in America and Europe. Among her most avid correspondents are
Victoria Ocampo and Alfonso Reyes, who also figure prominently in her *recados*.

There were approximately one hundred and fifty *recados* published between
1919 and 1951, and those in this anthology are dedicated to contemporary
women who had a strong historical presence. Gabriela Mistral dedicated these
pieces to women she read and women she loved. They are visions of shared
readings, such as her *recado* dedicated to Teresa de la Parra and expressions of
admiration, such as those dedicated to Sor Juana, Victoria Kent and Victoria
Ocampo. These *recados* allow us to appreciate the great degree of internationalism and transculturation found in Gabriela's clear and pristine pose. Her
attitude about women's contributions reveals an empathy with the works of
women, but also a strong preoccupation for the validation of those texts written by women. I believe that if it were not for Gabriela and the connections
she established with women in America and Spain, there would be almost no
information about the books they published. Mistral only published one book
in Chile, but she became the vehicle to create alliances and readings for
women. The *recados*, as well as her other texts, work to create a women's audi-

ence and to awaken an interest in reading. This is one of the most crucial aspects of the *recados:* to give a presence to the literary works of other women.

Mistral's *recados,* as Martínez points out, are filled with intuition; their prose is filled with sensitivity and, above all, her writing is authentic, without false adjectives. At the time when Gabriela wrote the *recados,* she broke all the norms. Then, one was only supposed to write about classical authors and important men. Gabriela wrote about the women's voices that were beginning to be heard, as we see in a *recado* dedicated to a key literary text: *Ifigenia* by Teresa de la Parra. Mistral is also a step ahead of her critics, who limited themselves to exposing, without revealing, the real "me" which arose from their readings and this is a laudable aspect of the type of discourse that Gabriela forged. Her discourse narrates her own history and feelings. In the artist's decalogue, Mistral says "You will give your work like you give a child, decreasing the blood to your heart." The *recados* acquire a new reading, one that feels like a dialogue and is always clear. Mistral elaborates a new way to make literary criticism which is similar to the essays and newspaper articles written by Virginia Woolf in the *Common Reader.*

During all of those years in which Gabriela Mistral dedicated her time to writing *recados,* she was always clear, personal and authentic, without allowing herself to be influenced by critics who judged her and criticized her for either personalizing her writings or being too archaic. Mistral continued to evolve and be part of the world and history, exercising a unifying role for women and their histories. She rejected the critic's comments and cultivated the *recados* as an intimate and deep relationship with what is written. Thus she created new disruptions and new ways to exercise her gift, her vocation.

For both admirers and repudiators of Gabriela Mistral, the fact that she was given the Nobel Prize in Literature is still cause for commotion in the literary circles of Latin America and Spain. Regardless of Gabriela Mistral's ambivalent feelings toward Spain, the Nobel Prize that Gabriela won was endorsed by the Spanish Language Academy and all Latin American academies. Gabriela was supported and backed by the more than twenty-one countries which supported her candidacy for the Nobel Prize. She first received this international prize and then achieved recognition within her own country. She never forgave Chile for this, and she continued feeling that it was the country of absence for her. Chile, and its writing community, was a male-dominated and exclusive country. To that effect, we only have to note how few out-of-print books by women writers have been republished through the years, the fact that few literary prizes are given to women, and the malicious and prejudiced criticism of women's literary works which was printed in newspapers of the time.

In a prophetic verse, Mistral stated, "And in a country without a name I shall die." Gabriela died in New York City and her remains were taken to Santiago de Chile. Her burial, as well as Neruda's years later, became a historical event at a national level and it defined the literary history of the country. The day Gabriela died was declared a national holiday and her wake lasted three days. This defined her importance in Latin American culture and, as Elizabeth Horan suggests, froze her in time.

Gabriela's image was comfortable and complex, according to the different governments which claimed her as their own. The right-wing governments, including that of Pinochet, desperate for a cultural image to show to the world, took Gabriela's image and made it into that of an abnegate teacher and a religious figure. In their paintings depicting Gabriela, she looks like a nun, covered from head to toe. Horan says that

> ...to honor Mistral became a ceremony of false tenderness which apparently recognized but falsely rejected poor children, agonizing mothers, abandoned indigenous peoples, the refugees and field workers. Her death told us clearly why this woman, one of the 20th century's greatest poets, preferred the anonymity of exile rather than living in a trap, constantly accepting the affronts of the daily bread of her nation.

Pinochet's government had dressed her up as an austere woman, with high-necked blouses. But during Salvador Allende's regime, the years of the Unidad Popular, Gabriela was vindicated. New, popular editions of her works were published. Her portraits showed her as a more beautiful and insinuating woman, with revealing cleavage. Once revived, Gabriela continued to be subversive. Even after her death she refused to remain silent, she refused to become part of Chile's hagiography, and she became a figure that the critics, especially the feminists, have interpreted differently.

There has always been a symbiosis between the figure of Gabriela and the national culture. Mistral is part of our history. She occupied consular posts throughout America and Europe, but as many have said, she has not been read broadly. Gabriela did not belong to an elite or to the landowners, but she managed to rub elbows with the most aristocratic families, with presidents such as Pedro Aguirre Cerda, and important senators, such as the Tomic brothers, in order to ascend to her position of power and maintain it. In this we see her greatest merit: the possibility of being part of power, but at the same time remaining committed to her causes, especially those involving women.

One cannot see Gabriela only as a poet, although her poetry is the most essential part of her literary work and her vision of the world. Gabriela is, above all, a wanderer, filled with unbridled curiosity. She says that she would write even on her knees and it was in that position that she wrote texts about Castille in which she imagined Mother Theresa wandering through the fields. She wrote *recados* about her, forging alliances between the present time, her view of Spain, and the past, framed by great figures who influenced her work. She wrote about materials, about bread, maize, sand and ashes. For her poems, extraordinary hymns of lyrical beauty, she chose the fauna of her beloved America or the tropical sun. Thus, Gabriela united with and gave voice to history and memory through poetry, prose and lyricism.

THE MILLENNIUM AND GABRIELA

At the beginning of this millennium it becomes more essential to incorporate Gabriela Mistral, not only as an artist, but also as an activist involved in the great transformation processes of this century. The final seven *recados* in this volume deal with women's issues, including suffrage, education, and feminism. Mistral represents the search for an identity, not through patriarchal power but rather through the minorities, the indigenous peoples and women, the search for an America without boundaries, an America that could reinvent and define itself. Among countries and cultures where the intellectual level is not homogeneous, Gabriela assumes with clarity and honesty her artistic vision, exploring the great questions confronting humanity: justice and the right to peace. Thus, she inserts herself early into the new millennium, adding to the Latin American cultural image: oral traditions of indigenous languages become part of her poetry, childhood traditions become part of her work, the vast Latin America territory is forever part of her work, and she does not forget the position of women but rather makes them ever present in both private and public spheres. In addition, she validates and gives plenitude to that other power women possess, a power which may be hidden, intuitive, and irrational but a power which is key in the organization of all social imagery.

At the beginning of the 21st century, it becomes more effective and necessary to revisit Gabriela Mistral's work and life and to incorporate her in the great post-modern currents of thought. The preoccupations of this wandering woman placed her at the center of an illuminating and far-reaching vision within the perspective of the great projects to vindicate women and children. Her preoccupation with women's and children's rights is not a cliché, but rather a progressive and defiant look at the status quo. One must then look at Gabriela not as the mother and educator, but as transgressor who, regardless of her humble social class and mixed blood, managed to impose herself on a chauvinistic, homogenous and conservative society. Gabriela Mistral, self-taught from foreign books, is above all else a woman who participated in the great movements of the 20th century. She fought for women's right to vote and created, through her role as a teacher, an important pulpit for educational reform.

Let's remember that in Gabriela Mistral's time, women's public voices were censured and relegated to a secondary plane. Gabriela carefully managed to play with this status quo and created for herself a significant and ever-vigilant pulpit. For example, at the beginning of her career, she received the support of great male figures such as Pedro Aguirre Cerda and José Vasconcelos. They granted her a voice and gave her a forum, always as a teacher. However, she defiantly turned it into a forum for women. She wrote for them. She prepared an anthology dedicated to them where the common and domestic intermingle with the importance of not allowing anyone to silence you. Mistral, from her early days in the Elqui Valley, was a great transgressor. Gabriela's humble origin and mixed heritage were ever-present in her mind, yet from that public forum, from the margins, she created controversies that won her fame as an anomalous, yet an enlightened and visionary, figure.

One of the most bizarre figures of Gabriela Mistral's iconography is the image of a dead woman who floats through a landscape both mythical and religious. It would seem that the Chilean culture is most comfortable with the image of the dead Gabriela, a woman of divine character. Curiously, while alive, Gabriela worked on the image of her death, but she did it in a subversive way through the dead woman in *Poema de Chile*, a woman who has fun and is happy because during her long trip through Chile, she finds her place. She speaks of flowers and animals and intones an international discourse, without borders. After her death, Gabriela became a subversive magician who spoke for both the living and the dead. The *recados* defy all the clichés surrounding Gabriela Mistral, who understood that her search for popular folklore and her roots were ways to hold a dialogue with her nation.

We hope this book will create a new forum for the reading of Mistral's works. These *recados* and political essays allow us to see an intimate Gabriela and they also permit us to observe a colloquial language, full of life; a language that is unlike that of her poetry and doesn't allow us not to pigeonhole her as a poor and oppressed teacher. Let these pages illuminate a traveling and sedentary Gabriela, a diplomat and a peasant, a somber and very clear woman; a Gabriela who drank scotch, smoked cigars and wrote poetry while on her knees. The *recados* are a universal and key aspect of Mistral's literary work. They show us whose books she read, how she viewed her contemporaries and, above all, how her writing was inseparable from her being and her life.

Translated by Monica Bruno Galmozzi.

GABRIELA MISTRAL'S *RECADOS*: MEMORY, RESISTANCE AND IDENTITY

JACQUELINE C. NANFITO

In recent decades there has been a renewal of interest in the essay, that hybrid literary genre which evasively defies definition, embracing as it does countless topics, approaches and modes of expression, including travel writing, confessions and memoir. This resurgence of interest and fascination with the personal or familiar essay, conversational and collegial in tone, as opposed to the outmoded, positivistic essay with its basis in argumentative, expository writing, has been associated with those cultural theorists and critics, particularly feminists, who openly question and assail the prevailing canonical modes and styles from which they have been excluded, those which have denied them language or inhibited the expression or representation of their selves. Among the principal objectives of the critical rereading of Latin American female-authored essays, such as the prose texts written by Gabriela Mistral, is the desire to rewrite the authorial canon and rescue these authors from their shared fate of absence, indifference and/or oblivion. Of equal importance is the need to understand Latin American women's prose writing as the rearticulation of the constructs of engendered identity and their desire to creatively write a utopian space in which to affirm the right to presence, as well as the right to representation of the other and the self.

Latin American writers, from the colonial days to the present, in the questioning of realities and the search for identities, have often courted and engaged the essay as a form that lends itself to the creation of uniquely personal visions and uncontestable worlds, given that experience is the authorizing force that anchors the essay, and that the construction of such visions is largely subjective. The Latin American essay evolved from the chronicle of Indies, those colonial texts of fact and fiction in which historical documentation was often combined with personal testimony—"lo visto y vivido"—and even the fantastic. In a seemingly endless search for identity, the essay has been employed throughout Latin America in an attempt—the very term *essayer* in French, *ensayar* in Spanish, signifies to endeavor, to experiment, to rehearse—to enunciate cultural identities: individual, national and continental. Since the beginnings of European colonization, Latin Americans have sought to define themselves and their cultural identity. One early historiographical text, el Inca Garcilaso's *Comentarios reales* (1609, is an epic revision of the history of the conquest of Peru, which corrects the "official stories" narrated by Spanish chroniclers by incorporating the mythopoetic vision of the Incan culture and restoring the Indian's place at the crux of cultural production and identity. Sor Juana Inés de la Cruz's autobiographical *Respuesta a Sor Filotea de la Cruz* (1691), is a learned treatise from the seventeenth century in which the Mexican nun defends for women and all individuals the right to knowledge and literary activity. The political writings of the Latin American intelligentsia of the nineteenth and early twentieth century, notably those by Sarmiento and Bolívar, Bello and Martí, Rodó, Mariátegui and Vasconcelos, were pivotal in instilling in the reader a national consciousness of shared identities, grounded for many in the concept of cultural hybridity. In the contemporary Latin American essay by vanguard writers such as Borges and Cortazar, the non-fiction form serves as a means of negating the coordinates of space and time and all human constructs on the map of reality and of postulating the existence of an other or multiple realities. For some contemporary Latin American writers, the essay has signified the means by which one may undertake the mythic reconstruction of history, as in the Colombian German Arcineiga's *América magica* (1961) and *El continente de siete colores* (1965),. In Octavio Paz's works, *Laberinto de la soledad* (1950) and *El arco y la lira* (1956), the poet has replaced historians and philosophers in the revitalization of myths from antiquity, thereby enabling the individual to reconstruct his past and recuperate his personal and cultural identity. For many Latin American women authors of the recent decades—the Mexicans Rosario Castellanos and Elena Poniatowska, Puerto Rican Rosario Ferré and the Argentine Luisa Valenzuela—the essay has lent itself to the charting of new courses for repre-

sentations of female subjectivities, to female identities other than those pre-
scribed by cultural mandates, heretofore largely invisible or silenced within
the realm of objective discourse associated with males.

Ever since the singular, solitary voice of Sor Juana first emerged from the
shadows of the labyrinthine patriarchal society that was seventeenth century
Mexico, defending in the *Respuesta* her right and that of other women to
knowledge, self-expression and all forms of intellectual pursuit, there has been
a continuum of female authorship in Latin America, often engendered in the
struggle to redefine one's roles in relationship to society, to others and to the
self. Among the first writers of this feminine tradition to emerge on the cultural horizon of twentieth century Latin America is the Chilean Nobel Prize
laureate, Gabriela Mistral, known to most individuals as a poet par excellence
more than as a writer of prose. Like her Argentine contemporary, Victoria
Ocampo, who ranks among the Latin American literary elite as founding editor of one of the region's most important journals, *Sur*, Mistral is one of those
few female essayists to be anthologized with the canonical Latin American
male writers of non-fiction. Like the aristocratic and cosmopolitan Ocampo,
Mistral also frequents the essay, that amorphous, protean testimonial form,
with its focus on the ontological self as it journeys, muses and remembers. For
these female essay writers, the self is progressively discovered, disclosed and
developed in and as discourse in the essay, coming into being through specu-
lative, ruminative expressions on the non-self, or the other. Whereas for male
authors, the fundamental masculine view of the self is of a separate, unique
individual in relation to the world and others, the basic feminine view of
women writers, most particularly autobiographers, is founded upon the
notions of identification, interdependence and community. The female subjectivities that are mapped in many of the prose texts of Gabriela, as a female
chronicler of human geographies and chronologies, are not defined in isola-
tion, but rather, in relation to others, through an interconnectedness with the
world.

The *recados*, a term which can connote varied meanings, from a simple
"message" or "greeting," to "complimentary regards" or "gift," to "outfit, tool
or implement," "daily supply of provisions" and even "abundance," were journalistic pieces, impressionistic articles, sketches, portraits, that Mistral published in several Latin American newspapers: *El Mercurio*, Chile; *El Repertorio
Americano*, Costa Rica; *El Tiempo*, Colombia; *El Universal*, Mexico; *El
Universal*, Caracas; *Sur*, Buenos Aires; *La Revista Bimestre Cubana*, to name a
few. Although several were composed in verse, the vast majority of the *reca-*

dos are prose texts that constitute a new genre in Gabriela's literary development as an author. Lamenting the lack of opportunity to maintain faithful correspondence with friends and acquaintances due to the increased demands on her time, the obligation to travel and fulfill her consular duties, Mistral invokes the *recado* as a forum from which to continue to educate the world on the wonders and woes of her beloved American continent, as she had been doing hitherto throughout her informative journalistic pieces, while simultaneously delving into expressions of the self. Through an expansion of epistolar expression from the merely personal, subjective rendering of realities recollected by the author to the more extensive commentary of geopolitical topographies and mapping of inter-subjective and cultural identities, Mistral successfully engages in interpretive discursive practices often inaccessible to women during the first half of this century. The engagement of the personal, experiential form of the *recados* allows Gabriela to poetically move beyond the journalistic cataloguing of epic events and achievements, characteristic of male autobiographical authorship, and embark upon the discovery and exploration of a discursive space in which to *ensayar* or rehearse the many versions of the other, and the self, in the examination and analysis of historical processes and social practices that condition and shape personal and cultural identities.

Accompanying the first of her *Recados quincenales* is a note in which Gabriela defines the *recados* as a kind of a generic letter destined for an extensive, more inclusive readership, with commentaries on newsworthy events and noteworthy individuals, from the epic to the pedestrian:

> I ask that you assent to this kind of generic "letter for many,"
> even though it is not intended for everyone, in compliance
> with the demands and needs of the journalistic profession. I
> ask that you kindly accept from me this baroque postcard,
> which is filled with commentaries of events both epic and
> pedestrian, with critical interpretations on certain texts, with
> that which we call "scholarly echoes," and, from time to time,
> tenderly harsh messages for my people: harsh, due to the
> forceful urgency to be heard, and tender, because of my love
> for these people.[1]

Throughout her literary career, Gabriela invokes the model of José Martí, whom she strives to emulate both in terms of composition and ideology. In his formidable, authoritative study of Mistral's prose production, *Pensamiento y forma en la prosa de Gabriela Mistral,* Luis de Arrigoitía affirms the influence of Martí upon Mistral in the formation of an instructional, educational journalism, the expression of an authentic Americanist voice on a multitude of topics, fueled and conditioned largely by concerns both moral and aesthetic.[2] It is through these writings in prose that she often articulates her most poetic visions of reality and of herself, as she authenticates herself in the prose on the page, essaying herself into being, a point made by Emerson and echoed by Lydia Fakundiny,[3] in the forging and fashioning of the self in and through the written word in the world of prose, in the observation of others, and of the self as reflected in the other.

Throughout her life as she charted new directions for Latin American women in the first half of this century, Gabriela left an indelible imprint of her personality on all with whom she came into contact, from the rural schoolchildren of her native River Elqui Valley, for whom she would improvise her verses with adroit facility, to foreign dignitaries and heads of state. It is an amazing odyssey, indeed, her journey from the desk of a self-taught school mistress, having been dismissed from the classroom as unworthy of formal instruction, to the throne of poetry, as the "spiritual queen of Latin America," the great singer of mercy and motherhood honored by the Swedish Academy with the Nobel Prize for literature in 1945. While no one would question the significance or the legacy of her poetic text, I am reluctant to concur with the opinion that Mistral's true world was her poetry, and that through the intuitive reality of this medium she spent a lifetime retracing those lost steps as a woman and a human being searching for identity.[4] A critical examination of the *recados* reveals the existence of discursive spaces that emphasize feminine experience and essence and the emergence of a feminist consciousness in the female poet's appropriation of an engendered literary tradition, the essay, in order to further advance the formulation of female identity.

Mistral, born Lucila Godoy Alcayaga in Vicuña, 1889, was first recognized as an author in 1914, when she was awarded the highest distinction for her "Sonetos de la muerte" in the "Floral Games," a juried poetry competition celebrated in Santiago, Chile. It is at that moment when the poet began to use her literary pseudonym, Gabriela Mistral. Gabriela was chosen for the archangel Gabriel, that divine messenger of good news, for Mistral identified herself as a child of air, as opposed to one of water or fire, distinctively blessed with intelligence and a spiritual grace;. She believed that she was destined to mediate between God and men as a creature of pure spirit and intellect.

Mistral is the name of the strong, warm wind of the Mediterranean, and also the name of a French poet who was awarded the Nobel Prize for Literature in 1904 and whose compositions reflect a love for his motherland, his native Provence, and the search for cultural identity, themes that surface constantly in both Gabriela's poetry and prose production.

In 1922, Gabrielaís first book of poetry, *Desolación*, appeared in New York, edited by the Instituto de las Españas (Columbia University) under the direction of Federico de Onís. It is also the year that Mistral left her homeland for the first time to move to Mexico, which will come to have a profound impact upon the development of her vocation as a literary artist. At the invitation of Mexico's Secretary of Public Education, José Vasconcelos, Mistral was asked to participate in the educational reforms of that country. Here she collaborated in the humanistic endeavors of the *Ateneo de la Juventud*–an important center of artistic renovation that promoted the concept of culture as a good belonging to the people–alongside Vasconcelos (author of *La raza cósmica*, 1925) and other great essay writers, such as Alfonso Reyes (*El deslinde, Ultima Tule, Visión de Anahuac*), and Pedro Henríquez Ureña (*Seis ensayos en busca de nuestra expresión*, 1928). Most importantly, the *ateneístas* confirmed for Mistral her belief in the importance of education as a catalyst in the process of social change. Furthermore, by inspiring examinations of national cultures and continental histories, in such works as the Argentine Ezequiel Martínez Estrada's *Radiografía de la Pampa* (1933) and José Carlos Mariategui's *Siete ensayos de interpretación de la realidad peruana* (1928), these epic essayists illuminated for her the powerful path of prose in the dissemination of significant messages, which would later translate into her *recados*.

For the majority of critics, as well as for most readers, Mistral is synonymous with poetry. As the designated "Schoolteacher of America," Mistral has been canonized as exemplar of the most lofty of feminine virtues, particularly those of chastity, magnanimity, and selflessness–ideals, extolled by the patriarchal order, which defined and constructed sexual and gender identities as fixed and stable cultural functions. At once Mistral was transfigured into the poetic representation of the intimate, interior realm of the passive, the sentimental, the intuitive, the irrational, but fundamentally, the maternal. This image was then appropriated by a nation whom she later came to represent as spokesperson in her consular capacity. Current feminist interpretation, nonetheless, posits the possible coexistence of multiple identities, in light of the complex, androgynous non-conformist aspects of Mistral's persona. The circumstances of Gabriela Mistral's life contradict her designation as "spiritual mother" of Latin America. Despite her own public career as poet, pedagogue, and diplomat, she often suggests a domestic, private, passive role for the intended *destinatario*, as in the intended female audience of her pedagogical anthology, *Lecturas para mujeres*. In a brilliant study that examines the issue of gender and *mestizaje* in Mistral's prose, Amy Kaminsky points out that Mistral lived most of her adult life as an émigré, despite her passionate Americanism; and that just as she lived outside a Chile for which she felt profound nostalgia, she lived a life that she did not affirm for other women.[5]

It is only recently that critics have seriously reconsidered the other Mistral, the prose writer, in critical re-readings of her essays that attempt to establish the relationships between gender and genre and to identify the coordinates of an alternate canon which, while maintaining dialogue with the established tradition of the male canon, transgresses established boundaries to chart a new site of female authorship in the landscape of Latin American culture. By virtue of the essay, with its characteristic openness, elusiveness and fluidity, Mistral is able to reconfigure the space of interpretive practice, once the exclusive domain of male writers within the context of Latin American patriarchal hegemony, in a willful reconstruction of the feminine to include public spaces of active production alongside those traditionally sanctioned inner private spaces characteristically associated with motherhood and reproduction.

The essay's shifting, porous nature proves to be the perfect discursive form for establishing a forum from which Mistral freely expresses her opinions as a literary critic and social/political commentator and reflects on a multitude of topics, including poetic musings on individual persons, places and objects, along with critical commentaries on contemporary events or political, social or moral issues. With its shifting generic boundaries and its coalescence of diverse, often opposing elements, Mistral's journalistic prose, which spans the years 1907-1957, the year of her death, serves as a means to construct and define this evolved sense of self as divine messenger and to chart new topographies of cultural identities and feminine subjectivities through the exploration and representation of others in the text.

Mistral, the essayist, appropriates the public sphere of male critical discourse by infusing the traditionally distant, overtly objective essay form with the informal, the intimate, the subjective, in order to engage in untraditional practices of interpretive power. In critical discourse, such as that of the essay, the critic's gender often determines whether a work is considered of broad interest: what is uncomfortably recognized as the subjective nature of criticism is seen as weakness in criticism produced by women, even though it is acceptable in the writings of men. Literary traditions have often favored national works over those with personal themes, and thus have contributed to the categorically inferior status of writings by women over the centuries, particularly in Latin America. It is important to point out, however, that for many of these female writers of prose, there was little or no distinction between the writing of objective history and that of personal histories. As Ruth-Ellen Boetcher Joeres and Elizabeth Mittman points out in the their "[An] Introductory Essay" to The Politics of the Essay,[6] it is really only in the past century that more women have begun to appropriate the essay as a form of their own. Prior to that not only were they rarely represented in the world of letters, but it was unfathomable that they should or could employ a genre that exuded experience, wisdom, and contemplation. These defining characteristics of an essay are most characteristically associated with male authorial power.

The canonization of Mistral as a poet engendered the necessary authorial stance, essentially spiritual, moral, maternal, of one familiar with the particulars of this world. She passed this on to the world via the vehicle of the *recado* or journalistic essay, from which she launched moral missives which took shape from the impressions left upon her through encounters with the other. Both as a poet and an essayist, Mistral's production characterizes her as a writer acutely aware of the social, political, and cultural problems of the mid-twentieth century, a time in which Latin America had recently incorporated the literature and culture of modernity. She engaged actively in protest and social criticism, often focusing on the material, symbolic and subjective situation of women and other marginal elements of Latin American society, as voiced in the following recado, "Sobre la mujer chilena," found in the chapter entitled "Chile o La voluntad de ser" in *Gabriela Mistral: Escritos políticos*, a selection of her prose texts:

> In Santiago, on the fringes of feminist meetings, women have forced open the wrought iron doors that were the professions: they are now cashiers in banks, and in the bookkeepers' ledgers no fraud can be found; they are doctors in hospitals and judges for juveniles. Their colleagues grumbled and growled upon allowing them to enter, and they now regret having displayed such ignorant contempt. Women are creative in narrative writing, brilliantly daring in the plastic arts, and fearless in the face of the most rigorous engineering and distinctive architectural projects. What these worthy

women still need, however, is for the farmhand and day-labourer to feel embarrassed when a woman sows or harvests and only reaps one half the salary paid to her male counterpart. What is incomprehensible is that the legislator still has no idea that this female employee typically works to support three children, and that these often are one drunken spouse or slacker and two of their offspring. Even more exasperating is the fact that until now one half of the population has lived on the margin of the cleansing vote that those mothers can exercise in terms of administration, and on the margin of the liberating vote that they can use to improve the lot of the poverty-stricken rural population.[7]

As a female essayist, Mistral directly intervened in the traditionally masculine domain of literary and journalistic production, thereby challenging established models of the role and function of the intellectual in Latin American cultural history and creating an alternate space for women intellectuals in the public sphere. Continuing the project of nation-building which had been ongoing since the days of independence in the nineteenth century, Mistral, like Ocampo and other contemporary female intellectuals of Latin America, brings a feminist agenda into her elaboration of a discourse that challenges and often overtly criticizes established paradigms of social space, official versions of history and sedimentary constructs of gender.

Mistral's prose is best understood in the context of the readership that she specifically addressed. The strength and beauty of these texts reside in her ability to identify and respond, as an equal, to the concerns of a newly-emergent audience of educated, middle-class women and to exploit the very language of feminine purity and genteel sensibility that had kept other women marginalized and silent. Borrowing conventions from biblical scriptures and from religious poetry and establishing parallels with religious exemplars and cultural icons of the male-authored canons further enabled her to legitimize her speech, a rhetorical strategy employed centuries before by a kindred spirit of hers, Sor Juana Inés de la Cruz, in her *Respuesta a Sor Filotea de la Cruz.* Throughout her prose production Mistral conveys to the reader a sense of women's roles as producers of cultural knowledge, working against their erasure within a still masculinist discourse on cultural production. Her prose texts open up a site for reflection on the role of women as active agents in the creative process and in the production of culture and for the articulation of authentic feminine identities.

The essay becomes a means of erecting bridges to unite distant, disparate entities; the reader of the *recados* is invited to sit back, as would an armchair traveler, and accompany Mistral in the museful exploration of uncharted terrains and the dynamics of a dialectic in which that yet unknown but always emerging continent of woman's being is in the making.[8] The itinerant Mistral, "a person somewhat errant, yet faithful to her paths," as she describes herself in her "Recado for Doña Carolina Nabuco," the Brazilian author of *A Sucessora*, had hoped to settle down in Chile, once retired from the teaching profession, and establish her own rural school with its own curriculum and norms, one born of experience and not that of "bald pedagogy." Upon her return from Mexico, the United States and her first trip to Europe, she decided to carve out of the Chilean space a place of her own, but she was unable to transform herself, as she declares, into a "stable creature of my race and my country." For Gabriela to come to full knowledge of herself, Mistral the intellectual recognized the need to view herself in terms of a stable other and the need to distance herself once more from her native country and the American continent which she dearly loved to thereby achieve greater objectivity in her gaze. For the self to constitute and define itself, she recognized the need to pass through the detour of the "other" and the disembarking on the shores of solitude, and for this very process to take place, one must seek and confront the other or if it is nonexistent, create it. In one of her numerous reflections on the virtues of travel, she remarks:

> Nothing penetrates our being without displacing something: the novel image wrestles with that which was already inside, thrashing away at the jellyfish in the water; afterwards, covering it gently like somnolent seaweed. Traveling is the profession of oblivion. In order to remain faithful to the objects that we come seeking, so that our eye receives them like a welcomed guest, with deliberation and spaciously, there is nothing more effective than the sweeping aside of others.[9]

The act of writing becomes for Mistral, consequently, a vital force or process, a locale to inhabit, as if the word were another world or the womb, a place of significant space for the conception and expression of subjective identity. Self-exiled and alone, in the service of the nation as lifelong consul, Mistral, without a permanent residence—homeless if you will—is at the same time, home-

31

word bound in the sense that she is tethered to the word, seeking company in discourse and residing on the page, resolved to inhabit the word and fashion a discursive means of reflecting on her own experience and that of others in terms of a critical self-reflexive relationship to the past, present and future.

Engaging in interpretive discursive practices most readily accessible to men during the first half of the twentieth century, Mistral expresses in the *recados* her views in an intimate, often autobiographical form considered more appropriate to women's personal expression, which simultaneously reveals the influence of cultural mandates and the complex relationship of gender and class to authorial power. Among the strategies and literary devices used in her prose to create the illusion of authority in the text is the disembodied narrative voice, the alternate use of the appearing and disappearing first person pronoun "I," which serves to mark the text with authentic, testimonial experience. The discourse employed throughout her prose provides the framework and methods for individual and societal transformation through the presentation of the female as an active agent in cultural production, the revision of patriarchal cartographies by the creation of alternative codes and signs, the emphasis upon dialogue as action and community as a viable and preferable means to personal development, the presentation of sexuality and the institutions of marriage and motherhood from the perspective of women, and the identification of the feminist with the struggles of all marginalized groups throughout the world, though most particularly in Latin America.

Published over a span of several decades, Mistral's *recados* represent an exemplary and influential model of female authorship in Latin America, one of the first conscious attempts by a Latin American woman writer to erase traditionally sanctioned boundaries of subjectivity to reconfigure the cartographies of cultural identities, thereby inscribing the feminine within spaces other than those of the irrational, the lyrical or the maternal. In the *recado* dedicated to the memory of Luisa Luisi, Uruguayan poet, pedagogue and literary critic, Mistral writes a moving defense of her recently deceased friend to counter allegations of perceived political transgressions. The text also serves as a platform from which to voice her own rejection of polarities and dichotomies, often associated with masculine behavior and discourse, and for the celebration of synthetic, syncretic modes, more genuinely authentic components of feminine identity:

Once, in Chile, crossing the Andean cordillera, I arrived at the famous place of the division of Argentine-Chilean waters, touching that magic place they call a border. There was no such Andean backbone, nor a separation of peaks. What I encountered instead was a stunningly capricious chaos of ascents and descents, and in the blindness of the immediate clouds, what appeared was an immense diffusion. Many times I have lived the same experience with ideological borders, above all with religious ones. But I have refused to remain there because of a stubborn will that makes everything vague disagree with me, and makes me detest whatever craftiness there is in the cloud and in doctrines without delineated contours.[10]

In this and in similar *recados*, Mistral reformulates the map of subjective identity, freeing the coordinates of engendered space to allow for the reconstruction and expression of authentic feminine essence and experience, for the emergence and exploration of worlds hitherto unknown or those waiting to be rediscovered, "lost within the folds of memory." The literary form most suitable to this process of discovery of self and others undertaken by Mistral is that of the essay, the *recado*, which most often translates into a missive of edifying testimony. As a communicative medium these prose texts serve as an epistolary bridge between sender and receiver, a means of intimate, interiorized communication that reflects an absence made presence in the evocation of a distant addressee. The focus of the reflection in the *recados* is both outward and inward as the author endeavors to establish a link between the other and the space of her own time with the aim of discovering and developing the self in the literary act of essaying on worldly events and individuals in an intimate, conversational tone. For Gabriela Mistral, the act of writing is an act of pleasure and of empowerment, as revealed in the description of the her poetics pronounced during a gathering of three feminine luminaries in the constellation of Latin American literarature—Alfonsina Storni, Juana de Ibarbourou and Mistral—at the University of Uruguay in the summer of 1938:

Writing tends to cheer me; it comforts me and always renews my spirit, regaling me with a day that is innocent, tender and childlike. Writing gives me the sensation of having spent some leisurely hours within my true country, within my particular habits, within my unlimited whims and fancies, within my absolute freedom. I like writing in a tidy room, although I am somewhat of a disorganized individual. The notion of order seems to furnish me with space, and this hunger for space is what possesses both my sight and soul.[11]

In view of the overall silencing of women throughout the ages, and particularly in light of Mistral's additional marginality in having spoken as a woman from the Third World, the reader of these prose "messages" is better able to comprehend Mistral's need to assert her authority as a testimonialist. Appropriating the space of essayistic prose once regarded as the privileged domain of male authorship, Mistral emits her missives from a subjective stance, evoking through memory the experiences of a life that is a past-made-present and a present-as-becoming, in the literary act of personal testimony, in the reflective act of writing oneself in relationship to others by means of the prose texts that constitute the *recados*.

The *Recados*

Translated by
JACQUELINE C. NANFITO

GABRIELA REFLECTS ON HER ABSENT MOTHER

Mother: In the depths of your womb my eyes, my mouth, my hands were created. With your richest blood you nourished me as one waters the bulbs of the hyacinth, hidden beneath the earth. My feelings are your feelings, and with this seeming loan of your being I wander through the world. Blessed may you be for all of the splendor of creation that enters me and becomes entwined with my heart.

Mother: Like fruit on a dense branch, I have grown upon your knees, which still carry the imprint of my body; another child has not erased that from you. You were so accustomed to rocking me that when I would run outside along the streets, you would remain there in the hallway of our home, as if saddened at not feeling the weight of my body.

There is no sweeter rhythm, among the infinite rhythms flowing from the Prime Musician, than that of your rocking, Mother, and of the peacefulness reigning in my soul, a tranquility attained in the undulations of your knees and in the cradle of your arms.

While you would rock me, at the same time you would sing to me, and the verses were nothing more than playful words, pretenses for your affectionate gestures. In those songs you named for me the wonders of the earth: the hills, its fruits, its towns, domestic animals, as if to house your daughter in the world, as if to enumerate for her the members of the strange family into which she had been placed to reside.

And thus I began knowing your harsh and sweet universe: there is not a single word for designating reality that I did not learn from you. Schoolteachers later merely echoed those beautiful terms which you had already revealed to me.

You brought me close, Mother, to the innocent things that I could grasp without harming myself—mint from the garden, a colorful stone—and I felt in them the kinship of all creation. You, at times, would buy me toys, and other times you would make them for me: a doll with eyes as wide as mine, the little house that would collapse at the slightest movement. But I didn't cherish those lifeless toys, if you recall: the one I most enjoyed, the loveliest toy of all for me was your body.

I played with your hair as though it were a confluence of fluvial strands, with your rounded chin, with your fingers, which I would lace and unlace. Your face, inclined toward me, was the entire spectacle of the world for me. With curiosity I would watch the rapid blink of your eyelashes and the light that would hover between your green eyes; and I was always awed by that strange phenomenon that would pass over your face whenever you were troubled, dear Mother!

Yes, my entire world was your face; your cheeks, like honey-colored hills, and the hollows that sadness traced toward the borders of your mouth, two small, tender valleys. I learned forms and shapes from studying your head: the quivering of young grass was in your lashes and the arching stem of plants in your neck, which, upon bending down toward me, encircled me in folds replete with intimacy.

And when I learned to walk holding your hand, attached as if I were an animated pleat of your skirt, I came to know our valley.

Fathers generally are too preoccupied with matters of consequence to be able to take us by the hand and accompany us for a walk down the road or to climb to the top of the hill. Consequently we are more often the children of our mothers, with whom we continue to be tethered, like the almond that is encased within its tight shell. And our most beloved sky is not that of the fluid, distant stars but that of your eyes, so close one can kiss them through their tears.

Father is off and about in the heroic madness that is his life, and we do not comprehend what constitutes his day. We only see that in the evenings he returns and customarily leaves upon the table a small amount of produce, and we see that he gives to you for the family wardrobe, the linens and flannels with which you dress us. But the one who peels the fruit and extracts the juice for her small child is you, Mother. And the one who cuts the flannel and the linen into small pieces, and then transforms them into a precious dress that hugs ever so tightly the shivering ribs of a child, why, that is you, Mother dearest! The most tender of all! The gentlest!

The child already knows how to walk and can also string words together like glass beads. You then place a brief sentence on the center of our tongue and it is there that it remains alive until our dying day. This sentence is as simple as the stem of a lily. But with it, short as it may be, we ask for all that is necessary in order to live anywhere in the world with graciousness and genuine simplicity: one asks for daily bread, one declares that all men are our brothers, and one praises the mighty will of the Lord.

And in this fashion, the one who reveals to us the wonders of earthly creation, as if it were an expansive canvas detailed with forms and colors, is the one through whom we also come to know the God hidden in all that surrounds us.

I was a sad child, Mother, a child shy like the nocturnal crickets in daylight, like the green lizard that imbibes the sun's rays. It was painful for you that your daughter did not play with the other young girls, and you would insist that I had a fever when you would find me in the vineyard, conversing with the gnarled tree roots and the slender, graceful almond tree like an enraptured child.

Now she is talking with you as well, though you are not answering her, and if you were to see her you would place your hand on her forehead, saying just as you would before: "My child, you have a fever."

Every teacher that came after you, Mother, only taught me what you had already revealed to me and would say with excessive words those things that you could express so succinctly. Their words tired our ears and diminished the joy we experienced in listening. Learning was far more effortless with you, just as it was to snuggle against your breast as a child. You would envelop me with your lessons, which were gilt with the wax of love and patience; you never spoke out of duty, and thus you never hurried, except when you felt the need to express yourself more fully to your daughter. And you never insisted that she sit still and stiffly on a hard bench, giving you her undivided attention. While I listened to you, Mother, I would toy with the cuff of your blouse or with the mother-of-pearl button on your sleeve. This is the only pleasurable learning experience that I have ever known, Mother.

Later on, I became an adolescent, and then a woman. I have walked alone, without the protection of your body, and I know that what they call freedom is a thing without beauty. I have seen my shadow fall, homely and sorrowful, over the countryside without your shadow by my side, dear little girl. I have also spoken without the need of your assistance. I often wish that, like before when I was your little one, your helpful words would find themselves in each of my phrases, so that my discourse would entwine with yours and together we would weave a garland of words.

Many times they have called me strong and assured, those men who do not know that the heart of a woman is always a straw eave, trembling at the fear of living. And upon hearing their words, I close my eyes to hide from them the entire truth. Because I feel that my head is much less steady ever since it ceased needing the support of your arm underneath it, Mother!

I have spoken among crowds of individuals and later felt discontent with everything that I said, seeing that the simplicity of your words has broken down in me, perhaps due to vanity, perhaps due to the foolish desire to give something profound to these obstinate men who, in order to comprehend, need a vigorously vulgar slap of a vulture's wing.

Of all the lessons that you taught me, there is one that I internalized most profoundly: that of returning something to someone. Thus, Mother, I have composed your lullabies and there is nothing I would rather do. Midway through my life I have come to understand that all men are unfortunate and always need a lullaby to soothe their weary souls.

Everything that I have thought uselessly, everything that I have expressed arrogantly, please disregard and do not consider seriously; instead, please receive from me those precious songs.

Presently I am speaking to you with my eyes closed, forgetting where I am so as to forget that I am very distant, with my eyes tightly shut, so as to not see that there exists a vast ocean between your body and my being. I am conversing as if I were touching your garments; I have my fingers slightly spread, and I feel that I have hold of yours.

I have already told you: I carry the legacy of your flesh, I speak with the lips that you made for me, and I gaze upon unknown lands with your eyes. You also see through them the fruits of the tropics—the mellow, fragrant pineapple and the luminous orange. You enjoy with my eyes the configuration of these other mountains, so different from the formidable one under which you raised me! You listen with my ears to the speech of people whose accent is more melodic than ours, and you understand them and love them, and you also tear yourself to pieces when at times nostalgia burns within me, and my eyes remain open yet unable to observe the Mexican landscape.

I give thanks on this day and every day for the ability you gave me to gather the beauty of the land as if it were water that one takes with the lips, and also for the wealth of pain that I can carry in the depths of my soul without dying.

To convince myself that you are hearing me, I have lowered my eyes and cast off morning, imagining that at this hour afternoon has befallen you. And to express to you all that remains to be said, the translation of which is lost in my words, I will continue to remain in silence...

(Mexico, 1923)

MOTHER: A MASTERPIECE

Love for one's mother, in my opinion, is similar to the contemplation of masterpieces. It is magisterial, with the simplicity of a portrait by Velázquez; it possesses the naturalness of a tale in the Odyssey, and also the intimacy, which may seem ordinary, of a page of Montaigne. There isn't any hysterical drama nor romantic fanfare on Mothers' Day. Its daily existence is similar to that of the prairie in the sunlight; in her, as in the agrarian plain, the planting and the harvest complement each other without gesture, within a sublime simplicity.

No one finds it extraordinary that women nurse their young. Maternal love, in the same fashion as a masterpiece, does not captivate its creator, nor does it frighten because of its ostentatiousness, its spectacle. That bowed sculpture of palm tree, fountain of milk that overflows silently two hours each day, never strikes us as being a source of pain. But let us remind the disrespectful one who passes by without a glance at the corner that a mother's milk is not separate from her blood but is the means invented in women to provide sustenance, and he who has not reflected upon this perhaps may find this somewhat unsettling... The blood of this person was given once as a donation to a sick individual, but never was it given continuously for eighteen months and in such an admirable fashion.

Nor is anyone amazed that a mother is vigilant and only enjoys sleeping half of the night. Man has stood vigil as a soldier in the barracks, spent sleepless nights as a fisherman out on the open seas, or has remained awake in watch over deceased loved ones at times in his life. The watchfulness of a mother seems something utterly natural to him, such as the loss of light at six in the evening; and it is because, without knowing it, man equates the pain of woman to all natural processes. It would only disquiet him should mothers, finally exhausted, break the cord of their habit. But neither the nourishing prairie nor the woman tire easily; that body which they call thin, of little bone and little muscle, and which they think is made for minimum work or for worldly parties, like the rush or the grapevine, resists weight and the thrusts of pain.

The onlooker also observes with serenity the mother of the demented child. Patience of that kind is similar to that of God, the lack of total repugnance in that creature; that this woman is capable of loving her beast, not as she would a perfect child, rather, much more so, all this is contemplated without astonishment. And, yet, what we see as a sort of aberration is a "pure miracle." To write the *Iliad* in a few years or to sculpt the head of Jupiter in a few weeks is far less important than to wipe away the drivel from the demented child day after day and be struck in the face by him. In mothers of this class I have experienced moments when I am left speechless and shivers run up my spine, because I have had the impression of touching the limits of nature and seeing the point in which the flesh opens and reveals in the wound a fire that blinds, that of the blazing cherub, who in the heavens represents absolute love.

And without going as far as that which is often related, without hurrying the misfortune, let us remember the common fact of the woman that raises average children, maintaining the attitude that the mother of Marco Aurelio must have had for the mother of Saint Augustine.

It is a matter of seeing in her the graceful beauty with which she serves breakfast to her beloved king with no expectations; of delighting in the care with which she combs and dresses him, lavishing him with the care with which she once treated herself. Moreover there are no words to capture the captivation with which she lives the entire day, decorating his room, smoothing the wrinkles from his rumpled clothes and restoring life to all that is worn by age. What clever resourcefulness spent on her precious little devil! The deceit of he who plays with gold dust unknowingly is always less fantastic than the deceit of the other who squeezes mud out of bare clay, mistaking the luster of mica for the sparkle of diamond. The mother of the demented child feels as blessed as the mother of St. John of the Cross. She would never think that nature had deceived her or that she was ridiculed by destiny or that she is watering a barren little fig tree which will not cast a shadow on her back because it is already destroyed by insects.

The mother of the incapacitated disregards the misfortune, and woe to whoever attempts to return her to her senses! From her chest emanates a stream of light which falls upon the poor child and makes him radiant; the strength that hums in her own blood assures her that her son is strong. If she read mythology, her own son would probably be Hercules, and if she listened to "Lives," her son must be none other than Marcelino Berthelot, being that he cannot be Madame Curie... Stubborn saint, eye with a girder of gold, musical shell that always hears a chorus singing, even though she may be the only one who perceives it...

Finally, no one doubts a mother's passion for her child, even though it is the passion that most endures. Twenty, sixty years on her feet, and this is not the product of sheer nature: the frenzy of the wind does not endure for long, and the fervor of the waterfall at times diminishes; the passion of the animal, weaker than that of the elements, is worth far less since it does not exceed the season. A mother goes far beyond nature in terms of loss, and she herself does not understand her miracle. An innocent women incorporates herself to the supernatural life by means of motherhood and it is not difficult for her—what a dear price to pay!—to comprehend eternity. Man can spare her the lesson about the Everlasting, which she lives in her crazy passion. Wherever she is, alive or dead, there she will continue to perform her duties, which begin with the day and never seem to end. The moment her child was born, she gathered the oars of the galley slave and embarked upon an eternal journey. It occurs to me that in the heaven of mothers there must be a place where there is no freedom, where servitude endures, only more pleasurable than that with which they lived while upon the earthly shell.

A mother's affection has the same absurdity as God's love for us. It lives, whether nourished or neglected. It never occurs to her to await compensation, and it would be difficult for her to show indifference. The burning bramble frightened Moses; but no child is alarmed by this other bramble which alongside him blazes without leaving a trace of ashes, the flame never wavering, broad and tall like the bonfire that flares when the entire ceiba or silk-cotton tree is ablaze.

Precious creature that embodies the gracefulness of the maternal spirit within an absolute naturalness. The genius fell to her chest, not to her forehead, but it descended in a torrent warmer than that of intellectual genius (light of the moon that at times does not produce anything worthwhile), and this genius became transfigured in her in humility, killing the pride that in men is the discriminating habit.

(1940)

44

SOR JUANA INÉS DE LA CRUZ

BORN AMID THE VOLCANOES

Sor Juana was born in Nepantla; the two volcanos delineated for her the familiar landscape; they revealed to her morning and prolonged for her the late afternoon. But it is not Iztaccihuatl, with its sharply pronounced contours, which influenced her temperament; nor is it Poppcatépetl, awkward in its ascent to the summit.

Nervo claims that the atmosphere of that village is extraordinarily clear. Sor Juana imbibed the refined air of the heights, which renders the blood less dense and the glance more guarded, and restores to breathing a light intoxication. It is a tenuous, marvelous air, like the delicate water of snowfalls.

SHE WAS OF GRAND GRACE

This light from the mesa opened those enormous eyes that they might absorb the vast horizon. And to enable the subtle movement through air, she was given that tall, elegant stature of hers and a stride that was like the delicate reverberation of unadulterated light.

Her village does not have the vagueness of vagabond mists; similarly, there is not the vagueness of illusion in the eyes of her portraits. Neither that, nor the overflowing of emotion. Hers are eyes that have seen, in the clarity of the mesa, creatures and objects delineate themselves with defined contours. Her thought, hidden behind those eyes, will also have a decidedly pronounced line.

Her nose and her sensuality. The mouth, neither sad nor happy, assured; emotion disturbs her neither on the outside nor within.

White, sharp and perfect the oval of her face, like a peeled almond; upon her fair skin the blackness of her eyes and of her hair must have sat sumptuously.

The slender neck similar to elongated jasmine; by which not one drop of oppressive blood ascended: the respiration felt smooth against it.

The shoulders, equally fine and her hand, simply miraculous. The hand alone could have remained of her, and we would have known her body and soul by it, as Gongoresque as the verse...it is beautiful, draped over the dark mahogany table. The learned manuscripts she studied, accustomed to having the yellowed, rugose support of older erudite scholars, must have been surprised by the freshness of moisture from this hand.

It must have been a delight to watch her walk. She was tall, perhaps to an extreme, it seems, and one recalls the verse of Marquina: "...the light rests extensively upon her."

THIRST FOR KNOWLEDGE

She was at first the child prodigy that learned to read, in secretive fashion, in a few weeks; and afterwards, the disconcerting youth, with a mind as agile as light itself, that left the courtly commensals of the Viceroy Mancera utterly astounded. Poor Juana! She had to endure being the dazzling entertainment for the learned tedium of scholarly men. Surely they were less interested in her concepts than her beauty; but there was Juana, responding to their twisted gallantries. The conversation of the salons was simply one more course in that elaborately baroque banquet that was colonial life: Inquisition, devout theater and intense chivalry. Juana had to entertain the old rhetoricians, answer their fastidious missives in verse, and in the receptions of the Viceroy, pass from the recital of an agile rondelet to the rhythmic sway of the dance.

Later, she is the sagacious nun, almost unique in that sheltered and somewhat simple world of the convents of religious women. How strange that cell with its walls covered with books and the table filled with globes and instruments for celestial calculations.

It is not true that, in the sublime Gongoresque nun, her inspiration was like a turbulent gust of wind; one cannot speak of the Muse exhaling impassioned palpitations over her temples. Her Muse is truth, an exactitude that is almost disconcerting; her Muse is exclusively the intellect, dispassionate. Passion, in other words, excess, does not appear in her life but in one form: the ardent desire to know. She resolved to go to God by means of knowledge. Beholding the whole of creation, she experienced neither astonishment nor awe, rather the pleasure of experiencing its many shades and contours. She yearned to know about the tremulous morning star. The marvel about her is that science did not lead her to rationalism.

She had, among others, this characteristic of her race: critical faculty, replete with cordiality at times but implacably observant.

A STING UNDER THE VEIL

Another characteristic of her people: irony. She possesses it keenly and attractively as if it were a small flame, and she playfully uses it upon others.

One need not be astonished at this alliance between irony and the religious habit. Saint Teresa also had it; it was her invisible shield against the very dense world that moved about her: imperceptive nuns that tended to be suspicious of the learned sister and to see the horns of the devil surface among the books in her formidable bookcase. They forgot about the other illustrious cells: those of the two Spanish Louises. But in the small and attractive bee, the sting is embellished because the same instrument that inflicts pain produces honey.

Sor Juana is so imbued with irony that she takes it from conversation and correspondence to her verses. Unlike the rosebush, where the softness of the petal is separated from the thorn, she puts the thorn in the center of the rose.

SISTER JUANA, GENUINE NUN

Then comes the last stage in her life. One day she is fatigued by astronomy, the vain expression of the constellations; biology, infinitely cautious and frustrated tracker of life; and even of theology itself, at times, a relative of rationalism. She must have felt, with the disillusion of science, a violent desire to lay bare the walls of the learned bookshelves of her cell.

She wanted to kneel down in the middle of that cell, with the desolate Kempis as her sole companion and with the flame of love for all knowledge.

She had then, like Saint Francis, a passionate yearning for humiliation, and she wanted to undertake the humble tasks of the convent that perhaps she had refused for many years: washing the floors of the cells and curing the repulsive illness with her marvelous hands, should perhaps Christ look upon her with disapproval. She wanted still even more: she sought the penitent's cilice and experienced the invigorating feeling of blood over her martyred body.

This is, in my opinion, the most beautiful hour of her life; without it, I would not love her as I do.

DEATH

She then contracted the repugnant contagion and entered into the zone of pain. Heretofore she had not known it, and thus she had been deprived in her experience of the world. The taste of blood, which is life, is the same salty taste of the teardrop, which is pain. Only now did the judicious religious woman complete her circle of knowledge.

As God awaited this hour of perfection, as He awaits the maturing in fruit, He then bent her over the earth. He refused to call her to Himself in the period of the undulating sonnets, when her mouth was full of perfect phrases. He came when the learned nun, kneeling on her bed, had merely a sincere, humble Our Father between her dying lips.

As she anticipated her era with a foresight so enormous that it inspired awe, she lived within herself what many men and some women live today: the passion for culture and sophistication during youth. Afterwards, the taste of over-ripened fruit in the mouth, and finally, the repentant search for that simple glass of clear water, which is timeless Christian humility.

Miraculous was the child playing in the orchards of Nepantla; almost legendary the brilliant youth at the Viceroy's court; admirable the learned religious sister. But magnificent, above all others, the nun who, liberated from intellectual vanity, forgets fame and verse and, hovering over the faces of those infected with the plague, inhales the breath of death. She dies having returned to Christ as the supreme Beauty and the pacifying Truth.

(Mexico, September 1923)

48

SAINT CATHERINE OF SIENA

She was almost a politician, this saint, somewhat a stateswoman, as we would say today. She is far less a mystic than our saint from Spain. Her kindness overwhelms me, like shallow waters, alongside Franciscan charity, which would expand the oceans.

But I want to relate the beautiful and dreadful episode of her life. Those were times when Italian cities were as jealous as women. Siena detested Perugia and in the worst moment of the rivalry, a young gentleman from Perugia fell prisoner to the inhabitants of Siena. Even though there was insufficient evidence against him, the very fact that he was from Perugia was sufficient cause for him to be condemned.

Catherine would follow, from the convent, the life of all of Italy. The verdict filled her with sorrow. As a Christian, the death of the soldier wasn't painful for her, rather his lack of faith, for which he was bound to die. She presented herself to him in jail to speak with him. This obstinate man, with his movements of resonant steel, looked at her as if she were the substance of dreams. Catherine was beautiful; a contemporary painter of hers has left a precious portrait: enormous eyes that extend to the temple; a mouth finely delineated; slender neck, and a hand which I have observed for infinite stretches of time, inexplicable in its marvelous perfection. Draped over her ethereal, attenuated body is the habit of the Dominican order, which is elegant in its simplicity.

She spoke with that characteristic persuasion of hers, which would soften even the most stubborn of Popes, and put impassioned anguish and fervent desire into her request. In her voice there was such an assurance of eternity, that the gentleman began to yield like the iron rod in the forge, conquered by unconditional kindness. He converted, receiving the sacraments, and promised to Catherine that he would enter penitent into the afterlife if she would sustain him in his last moments, accompanying him until the place where he was to be beheaded.

The day of the execution, Catherine was there. He looked for her among the mass of individuals and smiled when he saw those white garments and her inclined head. When the executioner placed his head upon the rock, Catherine looked at him anxiously, reminding him of his oath. He made a tender gesture of confirmation. And he doubled over gently toward the darkness.

Catherine received the head that flowed like those tremendous clumps of aquatic grass that we remove from a pond; blood bathed her chest; she was a veritable canvas of Veronica. She drank the blood with the veil of the habit inclined, with her hands, with all of her body. She looked at the severed head, looking for the expression of the mouth in order to know, and she found an enormous peace reigning over the countenance.

To understand the tremendous upheaval in her life during that brief hour, one would have to read that letter ("Of Blood") addressed to her confessor. I do not know of any words more intensely uttered by a woman.

(September 1924)

ALFONSINA STORNI

"Alfonsina is unattractive," they had told me, and I expected a face far less pleasing than the voice that I heard over the telephone, one of those facial expressions that comes to be something like a punishment given to the individual that exudes internal excellence. And when I opened the door and found her, I became disoriented, and I even went so far as to naïvely ask the question: "Alfonsina?"

"Yes, Alfonsina," she replied with a warm, amiable laugh.

Her head is extraordinary, not because of unflattering characteristics but due rather to the entirely silver head of hair which frames a face of twenty-five years. It is the most beautiful hair that I have ever seen: it is unique, as if it were the very light of the moon at midday. It was golden and traces of flaxen sweetness still linger in the whitened strands. Her watchful eyes, her upturned French nose, very elegant, and her rosy complexion lend a youthfulness to her appearance, which is contradicted by the witty conversation of a mature woman. She is small in stature, very agile and with gestures and a style completely her own, marbled (for lack of a better expression) with intelligence. She does not repeat herself, she does not languish, rather, throughout the entire day, she maintains the enchantment of the first moment of meeting her.

This is our Alfonsina. She possesses very little of us in physical terms, that is to say, very little American. I, who have a burning curiosity about race, begin to inform myself... Alfonsina surprises me upon relating that she was born in Switzerland, in the Italian Switzerland. Immediately following the declaration she tells me about her voluntary Argentineanism and her upbringing. We should say, rather, her Buenos Aires background, because there is nothing in her of the creole from the Argentine provinces. She is the new

American, that is to say, the blood from Europe grazed beneath our sun and with the generous eye for appreciating the bounty of the pampa; the future American, graceful tennis player, without the heaviness of the creole from Bogata, and a splendid, compassionate individual because her mother looked upon the Mediterranean and she receives the Atlantic in her gaze.

I spent seven days with her. I confess that I was somewhat fearful of the encounter without ceasing to desire it, because I passionately long for the very best in this world. Letters had drawn us a little closer together; Alfonsina, so unlike the typical American, who adorns herself epistolarily, had a reprehensible urge to leave her correspondents clueless. Perhaps it is a defense against the calamity that has come to characterize correspondence between literary figures. My Alfonsina, the interlocutor of our letters, was arrogant, playful, and, at times, willfully trite. In my apprehension of the meeting, there was no small amount of unexpressed fear. Within me there are unilateral interests; I am far from being the rich creature who, like the fertile earth, possesses a variety of elements and can give sustenance to many. Naturally, I feared, like the innkeeper along the country road, that my guest would not like my unsophisticated style, akin to an ungarnished meal of corn and milk.

The anguish was ephemeral. I did not speak to her about my own personal matters, which are of no interest to Alfonsina, nor did she speak to me about those which could make her seem eccentric to me. I have met few women so adept at human relations: she neither tired me with the importance of all that is hers nor did she leave me covetous by hiding it from me. She is more gregarious than Juana, who, being a genuine Basque descendent, is more guarded.

The entire celebration of her friendship is the result of her intelligence. Reserved in the expression of emotions, this actually acts as an advantage for her because while walking throughout the American lands, effusiveness ends up fatiguing, like an exuberant landscape. Profound, when she so chooses, without trancendentalisms; profound because she has suffered and she carries, like so few of us, the hollows of life. Happy, but not that multicolored tapestry of happiness of excessive folk, rather the elegant joy created from diversion. She is very attentive to whomever is at her side, with an attention borne of absolute understanding, which is, nonetheless, a form of affection. Informed like so very few others in this life, offering the appropriate commentary on the most diverse topics; a woman of the big city who has passed through touching it and incorporating it into her being. Alfonsina belongs to those who know as much cerebrally as they do emotionally, something very Latin American.

Simple, and yet, one must repeat, of an elegant simplicity, as nowadays there is a pervasive lack of attractive sophistication that satiates as much as excessive affectation, its adversary. There is in Alfonsina an absence both of naïveté and of pedantry and a confidence in herself that never translates into vanity, an assuredness of one who has measured one's strength in the face of a difficult life and is content with oneself. Smiling she says to me, and it accentuates this aspect of her, "*Alfonsina* means ready for anything."

There is nothing to say about the poet other than perhaps that she is the Argentine poet that one could place after Lugones. The most noble praises have been sung about her by distant critics, by those who do not exalt in order to annoy another nor to receive favors in return. She figures alongside Juana, an equally admirable author, with the legitimate authenticity of her exquisite poetry, which includes all themes, a varied poetry on account of its humanistic character, rendering it simultaneously merciful, cruel, bitter and playful. The extensive critiques of her compositions are exceedingly favorable.

With Alfonsina, I experienced the moment of most intense fellowship when she expressed for me the total admiration that we share for Delmira Augustini. "She is," Alfonsina told me, "the greatest of all of us, and we cannot allow that to be forgotten." It gave me infinite pleasure to hear that: we Americans are unaccustomed to giving due respect to those alive in our obsessive insistence on lauding the deceased.

"Yes, Alfonsina," I replied to her. "She was and continues to be the greatest, unquestionably the greatest. She is forgotten because our people still do not understand what could be called the observance of the noble dead: honoring them daily and loving them so that they forgive the flawed hand with which we gave them glory."

I have perceived about Alfonsina Storni the profound complacency that results from the discovery of a total individual in our new peoples, thereby worthy of an ancient race. But there is also something else: a woman who has fought with the disgusting wickedness of Life and who has the generous spirit of women who were served or of those who never needed assistance.

(Paris, March 1926)

TERESA DE LA PARRA

Teresa de la Parra must have been no more than twenty-six or twenty-eight years old. It is presumable that Minerva was like her and not the way that Phidias imposed her in the eyes of the Greeks, according to convention. The gods accommodated themselves to the body of their faithful with astuteness, and the Greek was swarthy, like people from the gateway to Asia at the tip of the cape. Her eyes, indeed, were green. She must have had more flexibility than what they gave to her. Less gravity, because if with one ear she heard the chorus of Aeschelus, with the other she was attentive to Aristophenes and the lighthearted poets. I believe, then, that Minerva resembled Teresa de la Parra, had only the sculptor not disfigured her in order to fashion her in the likeness of Plato with Egypt.

Teresa arrived at the gathering of South Americans in Paris, which typically was alive with heated animation in the realm of political commentary. Teresa would drop a Creole expression, extracting the conversation from the false quadrilateral of "principles." She would describe the ranch of Venezuela to explain the confections of the rural table—Abraham's table—which is that of the plains. The conversation twisted like a path: impassioned, it would become elegant and witty, transformed into something clearly South American, like the pheasant from the coast that emerges feather by feather from the mass of foliage.

Nonetheless, the one that creolized these gatherings in twenty minutes was a woman dressed by Paquin o Ducet, with ornamental gems made for her by the jeweler of the Rue de la Paix. Her hats could make Madame Sorel turn her head on the street. She delighted the boulevard with whatever she was wearing; inwardly she chuckled to herself, keeping it to herself. She was entirely

Spanish from Caracas or a daughter of the plain; she guarded her folklore in
a parcel and offered it whenever the opportunity arose; she had her Efigenia,
her Pastora, her Vicente Cochocho and her Daniel Vaquero all arranged on
the wallpaper of her bedroom.

She would not have acquired the even more South American gestures she
later gave us if she hadn't begun to silence the detrimental novelistic vein.

I know several of these "Frenchified" individuals about whom the storytellers from there speak. One of them is Ventura García Calderón, with Lima
and the Peruvian mountain range retired in his eyes, which lower themselves
down to the notebook as soon as Miomandre o Cassou leave him alone;
another, Toño Salazar, walks with Central America on his fingertips, and he
passes it on like a little salamander upon greeting me. Teresa is added to these
figures of a contagious Paris and a distinct America, which endured for them
for some time.

I continue with the probable similarities with...Minerva. It is possible that
she was, in spite of Euclidean geometry, somewhat popular in orientation, a
little inclined toward the very chorus of tragedy near the market of Athens,
and involved in the groups of ceramists. It is not an unreasonable venture to
suppose that in speaking with Homer the intellectual blindness made her
grandiloquent, yet with the women of the narrow streets of Athens she used
a popular jargon, interspersed with jokes. She then resembled the Venezuelan
Teresa that conversed with me in Paris.

Month of my saint's day, this April, and month of my saint's day without
my native landscape, which returns to my eye of forty years without an accent,
without my abandoning this roundabout, with foreign tongues reverberating
in my poor ear, and with a distant light similarly resonating on my skin, which
knows countries by impetus or by the severity of the sun.

It is to this state of longing for one's own that Teresa's book arrives to me,
the second, the finest.

Four years between La Ifigenia and Las Memorias de Mama Blanca and a
measureable leap in terms of skill, unlike any other in comparison with our
prose writers. During this parenthesis, Teresa must have enclosed herself with
her Spanish classics, above all with the anti-rhetoricians who are the best: her
Luises of prose, her Santa Teresa and her Arcipreste, in tight intimacy. It is
from there that she has emerged with this clean and facile Spanish prose, like
white clay, like that kaolin exuded by fine porcelain. That perfect language is
like blood in the uninterrupted sand-like flow through compact and compe-
tent veins, and that this blood is nourished noiselessly, one is reminded, from

time to time, by writers like Teresa de la Parra. She deceives the facility of the paragraph so that language assumes a natural function. This is not exclusive to experienced adult users of the language, as Teresa convincingly demonstrates that the dexterity that others have attained near their forties can also be achieved by those thirty-something.

All of this she does with ease, grace, and elegance not seen in Spanish feminine writing since our beloved Santa Teresa. Surely they will tell you that her wittiness is the result of her Gallic upbringing, yet another brilliant success of French irony achieved in a stranger. Quite to the contrary. It is the absolute playfulness of Teresa but more candid, uninhibited, because the Saint was always constrained by the severity of the profession, and we will never know the potential limits of the wittiness of her writing had she not become a nun. Teresa, the Venezuelan, has not had reason to be afraid of nor to spoil the ability—precisely feminine—and this is the advantage that she had over the religious Teresa.

Her laugh of the benevolent bee, of the bee that might have placed its sting in its own wax before it stung, doesn't produce a wound. One may wallow in it as in the trefoil, without injuring a hand. Not even a finger.

The description of María Moñitos, in the chapter in which Teresa entertains by making fun of herself and her companion—neither ill nor well regarded—is the most playful page that I have ever read. Soon it will be known among the scholastic "Literary Readers," delighting young girls approximately the age of Moñitos. But Cochocho stands firmly in the heart of the text. The laborer of a hundred trades, a doctor, water boy, servant and nanny, well remembered with affection by the storyteller, comes to be the definitive stamp of the work, even though the other images that she has cut from her ingenious memory are likewise as admirable. (There exists a memory of genius because it is dynamically synthetic and precise; the other, the minutely cautious and dry one, is the commoner of memories, the little memory).

One sees Cochocho cleaning the flagstones; as he bends over, one touches the uncombed hair atop his head, which resembles a blackberry bush; when he moves, one smells the rural odors of the countryside, one celebrates his bigamy, like a residue from Abraham...in Caracas. Let us state without faltering that the physiognomy of this plain-dweller is a masterpiece of the creole genre. Clarification of the adjective: three literary creolisms I see with regard to America: one very clever and compact, like the head of Cochocho, with earth, rye-grass and thistle; the first born of Martín Fierro, who sustains like the pampa or plain all that which is fine and coarse (just as Shakespeare did not remove from his texts certain topics), and the creolism of Teresa de la Parra in this chapter, which offers itself in a language more perfect than the other, without perfection, signifying here prudence. This prose of Teresa reveals a controlled spontaneity, like that which demands the new pedagogy.

With grace and facility, the tone ends the theological triangle. The marvelous tone snatches the reader in the prologue and doesn't release him until the end; it has cajoled him, flirted with him, delighted his ear without fatiguing him in three hundred pages.

Totally aware that tone is her commanding strength, Teresa praises what she has, without vanity, as vanity is to sing the praises of that which is still in the process of becoming....

"If I were a novelist," she says, "before beginning any dialogue whatsoever, I would always extend a musical staff over the page. To the left, as is customary, the clef, tone and meter; then the spaces and bars upon the musical stave with notes and intervals, and underneath the text; the same as for the song."

The tone of Teresa's work is a combination of folklore and classicism, or rather, innate simplicity entwined with distinctive elegance. I look at her gazing from behind the paragraph in a striking twinship, the head of Perrault with that of Fray Luis of Granada. With that pair of individuals she succeeds in exceeding limits. May she never lose it, nor let go of it from now on, since she has masterfully entrapped it.

Teresa has made me think about the paternal lines of the tone. Unity of tone is achieved in a work when it has ceased walking—road, influence—and the writer has sat down with acquisitions suited to her intimate, intuitive liking. She is a master of language; the enterprise of requesting here, acquiring there has been resolved.

All this speaks about the tone in general. And now about her. How has she achieved such a uniformity of tone amidst the magnificent clamor of Spanish and French voices that danced in her ear?

Her profound understanding—wise one that you are, Teresa—has safeguarded her from adopting two or three of them; in the same fashion it has helped her to avoid tones foreign to her people. Unlike our Frenchified Latin American compatriots Gualligaica or Puno, she knows that neither the tone of Giraudoux nor that of Valery will assist her but only that which, on the Venezuelan hacienda, she absorbed with the milk, the guayaba, the creole sweetmeats, and with the adventures of Cochocho. She has come to realize something even more significant: that the American creature is the result of the confluence of city and country, and that American literature should also emanate from this very conflux.

During the ten years of living in France, the characteristic "abandon" of ours had been dampened though not lost. She has succeeded in reviving it, just as Cochocho does with the plants among the flagstones. No one else would be so loyal, Teresa.

I am not certain that in Venezuela they are aware of the stature of the novelist that has been born to them, and if they are pleased or not by the abnegations of this art, which bends like an arch over their county, intertwined in customary fashion as is the mistletoe with the Chilean poplar, by means of tenacious shoots from the roots.

If not today, tomorrow or someday...

As for myself, I can say that I liken the language of this author to the artist of the Flemish altarpiece, a mature individual but with a sprightly hand, each time raising a toast. This prose is the last reddish apple that the artist gives me to relish and I bite into it with passion in the pleasure, Teresa.

(Paris, May 1929)

THE LAST CASTS

The second Teresa de la Parra was born in the Swiss mountains, the one that her friends on this side of the shore and those on the other would never know, and one that I personally kept under my eyes for ten months out of incessant consolation for my grief and, who knows, if for some significant change within myself.

Teresa de la Parra was now looking for life without sensuality whatsoever, and she did it in a special and secret fashion. "That which saves me may be of importance, but it also has no special importance for the sake of my soul."

The soul, like absolute vision, had revealed itself to her on the alpine mountain to a point that renders one speechless, because it is here that we cannot offer anything less than the bundle of air from Grace.

Teresa de la Parra was speaking of great events and of domestic trifles from a special center or axis, and it didn't matter if the theme was serious or trivial: What had changed were the tone, the attitude and the disinterest. It made you want to ask her what experience she'd had in the days and nights of the foreign sanatorium. Her answers, at times evasive, at times whispered in confidence to me, I count among the priceless things that I, myself, have come to know of the ineffable in this world, where nothing matters to me as much as this type of news.

Lydia Cabrera must be able to tell those friends of hers about this quiet and definitive industry in the transformation of Teresa, the worldly woman, for the Teresa governed by a divine and silent command.

Between small bites of bread and little sips of coffee that she enjoyed serving me from her hand, I lowered my eyes and cried silently to myself. She seemed like a saintly queen, Isabel of Hungary or Isabel of Portugal, helping her inept cook or attending to the table. One had a string of intuition with respect to her secret, seeing these and other great acts of humility of hers; they burned suddenly because of what they possessed from another realm, and I, upon receiving them, felt something like a chill of shame.

She knew how to live her youth to the fullest in the blush of its ripeness, unlike so many other young women, without miserly reductions but always with a perfect decor; she knew how to live her adult life threatened by a terrible illness yet with a stoicism free of bleakness, and she knew how to endure her death, thrust into those realities of the spirit where she could see well like those "who had eyes to see."

Magnificent and beloved creature, to help her on occasions seemed an earned privilege and on others, a useless task. No service, nor religious conversation, nothing within our means was of any help to her, whose body in two years on the mountain had been whittled away by the thin edges of the hidden chisel.

I cannot designate with one name or another the invisible tool that disfigured her in those years of alpine solitude. It suffices for me to know that this devastating blade exists, the lick or stroke of fire, because I saw it and felt its triumph over that individual within the stretch of my hand.

I knew what I am talking about in a vague way and yet, with certainty. When she arrived to my home in Lineal City, I made her comfortable in a chair or bed, arranging the Guatemalan or Mexican sarape over her now hunched back or over her chilled legs, with the aim of gathering together things of ours, believing, like the Indian magician, that the only thing that helps us with its emanations is that which is authentically ours, that which is made or comes from the place or circumstance of our kindred.

I cannot relate to the curious individual who reads, with the objectivity that he would like, the "way of Teresa." The blessed die of spiritual principles that one rolls through the hands. It is probable that there was no novelty in all of it in terms of doctrine, as there isn't in many Christians or in every Christian to whom suddenly light shines above his head and in front of his footsteps. However much one knows becomes even sharper and more precise; however much one had recited in the lap of one's mother or in the nave of the church, suddenly takes on a tremendous vivacity within: one begins to live Christianity from the depths of the soul to the marrow of one's bones and nothing else occurs, this being a transformation of self.

The natural nobility of Teresa, terrain that she always inhabited, had become a kind of broad civility that now embraced peoples, friends, enemies, landscapes and animals. She was arriving at the total conciliation that in most is produced on the verge of death but that she experienced much sooner, and it wasn't the observing or somewhat aesthetic sympathy of the delicate souls that arrive here by measured discipline, rather a vertical illumination, a tearing away of our intimate skin. Her understanding, which always insisted upon comprehending in order to justify seemed now to apprehend each event, each case, by means of an illuminating lightning bolt, and to respond to that seen with an immediate act of her new reasoning. The eyes of the wealthy woman had been forced open at the sight of the misery of the world, and the hunger of the Hispanic people, the last spectacle that she viewed, which caused her great affliction. Senseless injustices disturbed her most profoundly. The last text of hers which I read would be a letter that she wanted to send to some friends in Bogota with regard to a particular manifesto written by some Catholic women, in which some sad commentaries were made with respect to the diplomatic activities of Palma Guillén, whose exemplary Christianity Teresa knew as well as I. (I did not allow her to send her astonishing protest, to avoid her involvement in the ridiculous dispute.)

Previously she found wickedness repugnant, now it made her infinitely sad. She could hear the world outside Europe wail because of the blindness of the mighty and the confused anger of the hungry. And she would cast her eyes, along with mine, toward Latin America in anxious search for the "day after tomorrow"...

At this stage in her life, Teresa seemed to me such a precious creature that I would follow each small action of hers in order not to lose anything. Like the Japanese painter who wanted to capture his sublime model from her manner of eating to the way she turned her head, I would follow her from the hand that peeled the orange to her childlike laughter at the ample mestizaje, or creoleness, of her visitor from the plains.

REMAINS

While vacationing in Lisbon, I remained haunted by the images of this second Teresa; I still was believing in the skill or the ostentation of the latest doctor when the telegram arrived from my Cuban friend informing me of the defeat. The notice arrived on a day of debilitated health, the result of a night filled with those tics from the air and light which overtake one without leaving a trace and come out of nowhere. I do not believe in such signs, at times deceitful and always futile. If these are signs, why are all of them so uncertain? And, if they do come, why does the air remain devoid of them at other similar moments of crisis? Teresa came, Teresa did not come. It was the time of her agony. The critical moment was already past.

As always I never came to a complete understanding. But what I saw clearly and what disconcerted me is that at that precise moment we suddenly lost an individual who had crossed the farthest reaches of the soul's southern zone to help the rest of us with what she had just learned, invalidated in the time of her ability to aid us in our confusion.

At birth our bodies and souls sign a vague contract with the earth: the one gives the robustness of the good slave, Aesop; the other offers an infinite well that will replenish with overflowing pitchers. The slave works forty years, receiving very little generosity from the moody nymph, until one day his bucket hits upon an unforeseen vein. In that moment of epiphany of his profession as man and water-bearer, precisely at that conjuncture, the slave falls, dissected by the urn of air he was needing and by which he is choked and overpowered. It seems like the absurdity of a potter who breaks the potter's wheel; it seems like the bewilderment of the lamplighter who does not accommodate the rough deposit with the airy lampshade. Then we feel, those of us who see, the calamity, the depreciation of life in general and of our own by extension.

Just as it was a joyous ritual to eat melon and Spanish bread with Teresa, hearing her sing the praises of each morsel of bread and slice of sunshine; just as it was a delightful act to extend water to her dry mouth, eating, walking and breathing became completely insipid and unspeakably unattractive after her definitive withdrawal.

In the profession or penalty of writing, where inexpressive or inadequate words cause grief, these very words now open up a barrage of expressions of consolation.

The term "withdrawal..." It's almost like saying "conveyance," almost insinuating a loan of sorts. "To whom and what kind of transaction?" I ask her, knowing fully well that she will not answer me, that this time I no longer have recourse to an answer, not even that courtesy of hers, the flower of her nature, that I called "natural and supernatural."

RESTITUTION AND RETURN

The only real debt that I owe to the Hispanic woman from Santiago who made me leave Madrid is the loss of the last days of Teresa de la Parra, which I was unable to experience. An unforgivable folly is to blame for the fact that I wasn't with Lydia Cabrera, combing that dear head for the last time, that I didn't put my *mestiza* hand over the casket, the foreign rock and soil that compressed and received her form.

In niche number 101 of the West Cemetery, Teresa de la Parra awaits her transit to the American *meseta* which gave here a marvelous childhood.

To Rómulo Gallegos, her older brother in the story of America, and to the women of Venezuela, I implore you to assume the task of preparing this return, of which she most certainly would approve, wherever she may be, and which will bring her pleasure, wherever that may be had. Whether or not there is resurrection of the body of physical kinds, it is important for each individual to respond to the call from his natural cell and his legitimate tomb, and those of Teresa are the soil, mud and rough stones of Venezuela.

(October 1936)

MARTA BRUNET

Within the past five years we have experienced an expressly effective enrichment—and of what tacit formation!—in addition to and alongside that which Pablo Neruda has brought to us. We have received (and here I place immense tenderness and joy in the participle) the most genuine gift, the contribution of Marta Brunet, the Chilean novelist from Chillán, whose legacy is so authentic that one can almost touch it, as if were the attractive lime tree growing by the river.

I will proceed to enumerate those elements which constitute our cultural values: folklore, which is an American mine that only the Chileans have worked with dignity; and novelistic prose, which presents a richly varied composite, that beginning with Barrios, Maluenda, D'Halmar and Edward Bello, passes through Prado, Contreras, Latorre and the Labarcas, and continues on in the works of González Vera, Rojas and others. Our literature follows a spiritual journey entirely contrary to that of the rest of the continent, which produces poets before prose writers, even though they may already possess the distinguished names of García Calderón, Reyes, Fombona, Quiroga and others.

Marta Brunet came upon us "fortuitously," as we would say in our part of the world, without scrutiny—the *pinino*, or shaky first steps, as Silva might say—so unpleasant, yet so natural for others...without having passed through the magazine, a source of advertisement for this or that well-endowed adolescence. In his introductory article, which I accept entirely with the exception of the following assertion, Manuel Vega insists that Marta's formation in her province was with her Spanish classics. I beg to differ with such paternity. In

63

America, more than anything readers of the Spanish classics borrow stylistic devices from those texts (even though they could also very well take examples for narrative construction). Generally they learn mannerisms. In Marta Brunet, style is unimportant, just as it is in the writings of Dostoevski and in the majority of narrative constructs. On those occasions when she is compelled to produce a "strikingly beautiful line," her efforts are futile as the sentence doesn't mesh with the rest of the text, sounding forced and unauthentic. Her reigning success, her greatest triumph, is the creation of Chilean characters that she brings to life for us. In this vein, which is neither greater nor lesser than that of the novelist, I am convinced that no one surpasses her. Perhaps I am mistaken, not having read the more recent Chilean novels; but as I recall, I am unable to evoke from memory those types who enter with such compatibility into the family that she delivers to us in her prose: her Don Florisondo, her Doña Santitos, her María Rosa and her Meche.

There in the province, as a good assistant throughout the first period of literary formation with her "excess of time" and with her air of indifference toward the writer, which translates into a useful gift of serenity, Marta Brunet has ingrained herself, has ploughed a place for herself, nurturing herself with Chileanisms. She has appropriated all things Chilean: the landscape, accent, customs and character. Reading her prose, I feel that to a greater or lesser extent almost every one of us comes from either one text or another, to which we cling with the hooks of emotional coincidence. Rojas, from the Russians, D'Halmar, even before that, from Loti and so on with the others. In Marta's text, one never observes the familiar hand of the teacher who assists and sustains. It simply comes from her ingenious talent for observation, an observation that is not that of watchfulness or a vigilant stance but almost the inhalation of the phenomenon. It is in this way that she absorbs reality in its entirety and delivers it unerringly. If she has made me remember Gorki and Introit it is not due to the style nor the twist of the narrative line, nor because of the form of lancing the subject matter—if the taurine noun is permissible; it is because of the astonishing creation of character. For me, Don Florisondo has a certain way of walking and even a hoarseness; I see María Rosa walking along the Chilean landscape without tiring, embarking on her healthy adventure, even a little aggressively. This difference extends to the types sketched a la Zola and to those fashioned in the style of Gorki, that is to say, those who are formed from a compilation of details, piece by piece, and those who are created as if descendants of Adam and Eve. The first characters reside in a few principle scenes of the story; the others are never cut off nor buried in secondary chapters, the initial breath keeps them active, alive from head to toe, throughout the entire text. If it weren't so wrought with use, I would venture to employ the expression that Marta does not construct but rather invokes her characters. Clearly in her case there is something magical.

When I undertake a rereading of her work, I generally experience a truly satisfying adventure. The narrative becomes dramatized for me, with its many moments of tremulous excitement; and in spite of our tremendous differences in temperament, the novelist and I seem to merge in the genre of the melodramatic tragedy of *The Daughter of Jorio*. I insist that this transformation gives me immense pleasure because the works that I most love have always transfigured me in a similar fashion. From *The Divine Comedy* to Dostoevski, passing through Hardy, Balzac and Maupassant, to name a few, the texts that have touched me the most are those which have thrust themselves onto me and totally engaged me, perpetually transforming into drama. On the other hand, I am not a believer in the rigid division of genres according to rhetorical norms. Marta Brunet has forced me to confront her Chilean rural with my own. I also recognize them, and even in those cases when I could or would not subscribe to a particular one in a story, I believe that I can recognize in them a genuine authenticity. They are for me what they were for her precious eyes: somewhat tender, a trifle ferocious, almost always savage in love and in boredom; pure upon the surface of their instinct, and, from time to time, absolute masters of a singular gentleness that emanates from the naked stone of their strength.

I am a country girl by blood with observant eyes and know that the most touching tenderness is that which emerges spontaneously, unexpectedly, from the strong and often cruel individual, astonishing whoever discovers it.

The adoption of an orphaned child by Don Florisondo belongs to this tender gesture of the *camallo,* or the arrogant, quarrelsome farmer with whom I am most familiar. The brutish beating that María Rosa inflicts upon her lover is as Chilean as the Llaima, and even more than that. But this María Rosa, might she be the "fearless woman" of the country, as we say more colloquially in those parts? I also have recognized her in the cities, and she almost crystallizes into a symbol. Our women can be found there as well, endowed at once with fortitude, wrath and mercy. I see her in myself with an identical contradictory nature. The day shall come when a muralist, much in the style of Diego Rivera, who compiles legitimate symbols not only from history but also from the grand narratives that we have attained, will put this María Rosa, the half cousin of Fresia, in his theory of the definitive creatures that have given birth to us.

Beyond the artful forging of types (I wish to rephrase: the brilliant forging of characters), Marta Brunet possesses, in spite of her blood whose half we share, a distinctly Chilean sobriety, an inexplicable earthiness, and a direct, often brusque mode of that is characteristically ours. Perhaps I am coming across as overly patriotic here. Yet it is certain that other writers loyal to the rural genre speak in this fashion, just as she does, invoking images of country life.

How is it that the rural narrative has settled in her to the point of attaining mastery and adeptness? I believe that perhaps she was one of the storytellers that abound in our country before she began her writing career. I smile at the memory of one of them who was a prodigious mother, endowed of grace and deeds, in the valley of Elqui. Or perhaps it was her mother, or simply another more cultured, rich and all, who has willingly listened to the sound of shepherds and woodcutters, as recommended by Maragall. From Maluenda, another colleague of hers, I remember a magnificent gift of storytelling, which I have never forgotten even though I heard it twenty years ago.

In the three years elapsed between *Don Florisondo* and *The Flower of Guillén*, Marta Brunet has not lost her touch at skillfully sketching and sculpting narrative types. The latter is clearly the superior of the two, and I expect it to rank among the finest American rural novels. One day she will arrive to Spain celebrated for her work to pronounce to those who understandably have bemoaned our vast void of autochthonous stories: "Here is something that has never been done in the either the land of the gauchos (despite Guiraldes) or that of the indigenous peoples."

There is, yet, still another success in her work: the artful handling of the grotesque. The elderly Doña Santitos rubs elbows with Goya. Perhaps owing to its brevity, this narrative has been very little celebrated. We're fond of making a novel out of a short story, a genre that we have tended to underestimate and mutilate in the transformation.

I have been, and still am, one who enjoys the elegance of style. Ortega y Gasset's prose gives me infinite pleasure, as one delights in pre-eminent tapestries stitched with linguistic threads and embroidered brocades of the tongue, ascending along the same lines as the prose of Flaubert but without ever losing interest. Marta Brunet has won me over without overindulging me with aural or visual pleasures. Metaphors are virtually absent; as are arduously wrought verbal weavings; one merely finds her extraordinary rustic mural of characteristic types authentically rooted in the Chilean landscape.

Don Pedro N. Cruz has suggested that she abandon the narration of rural topics and direct her energies towards others. This does not strike me as sound advice, despite his experience and wisdom in the profession. When an individual has been blessed with the supernatural gift of creation, be it a miner as in the case of Lillo or vagabonds as in the case of Gorki, "why discard that which teems with life in order to enter into the hotel of M. Bourget or another similar sort, where the air is already so confined."

With regard to the judgment of others, I subscribe to one of their opinions but with the best of intentions: that concerning language. Marta Brunet's characters possesses sufficient vitality to transform them into scoundrels if given an ordinary language. I can appreciate regionalisms in terms of collective phenomena of fondness for the landscape, for the customs, in the domestic realm, at times in the architecture, and even in the traditional clothing. But I detest regionalisms in language.

With a modesty bordering almost on the irrational, Marta Brunet seems to have wanted to write exclusively for Chile, or even more so, for her own province. It happens that even I am unable to understand several of her colloquialisms. I can only imagine that in Central America or Uruguay the reading of her texts must be disastrous owing to the unbridled use of dialect, which she has employed with such disdain for the foreigner that she hasn't even placed a line of vocabulary in the footnotes. In Chile we must have at least four regional languages, if not more. That of Coquimbo is not the same as that of Chillán, of course. She set out to recall that in Latin America, popular speech creates absurd linguistic differences, that the word *guagua*, for us means "small child," in Peru, it refers to a bus, and in Mexico, it is the name that children give to their dog. Another example is *choclo*, which means "shoe" in Mexico, whereas in Chile it is an ear of corn.

She ought to abandon that form of creoleness, which is self-defeating as it limits the scope of her reading public. A. Ramuz in Switzerland sins for his part, yet only venially, by writing his admirable novels in *patua*, yet never daring to venture as far as she does. She should not senselessly waste the field that her literary destiny has given to her in the Spanish language, a language magnificent on its own, and that, additionally, ranks third in the world because of the vast extension that it embraces. Divesting her characters of the crutch of that horrendous Chilean rural jargon will not in any way diminish them in terms of their authenticity and human context. I am not advising her to follow the examples of Frederic Mistral, marvelous epic poet along the lines of Goethe who has been reduced to being a great French poet because of his reckless similar loyalty to Provence. Such allegiance to the small motherland brings tears to the eyes because of the tone of humbleness with which it is charged, yet it also irritates.

May you receive this reproach without bitterness my brilliant, extraordinary and beloved Marta Brunet.

(Paris, June 1928)

NORAH BORGES

Recently in Madrid the Argentine, Norah Borges, held one of her exposi-
tions. There, surrounded by her drawings, we saw the one who is, even phys-
ically, the mother of her imaginative creations: there amidst her family of
extraordinary cartoons, and we can no longer see her in any other manner
than as she was at that time.

Where had Norah found such aptitude that allowed her to formulate this
kind of obsession? She surely prefers children in order to place them at the
table; to extend their bodies over the sand where she was able to plant more
little ones, only to then dismiss them, so that we might derive pleasure from
their sculpted bodies. Even more frequently, they rush forth to meet us in an
unexpected encounter, impetuously, with those enormous eyes wide with
wonder.

Norah has not seen more children than I have, yet, unlike me, she has
observed only them and chiseled her other-worldly figures as if they were shadows. She will not see anything but children until the day that she dies, at
which point she will arrive at another life narrating the tale of a curious planet
of her own invention, one on which no one has been harmed throughout the
course of his or her life nor has ever died of grief. She has had the good fortune of playing the role of King Midas through an alternative means.
Wherever she placed her hand an infant leapt to her breast; wherever she cast
a gaze, to her sheer delight a young child would arise to be painted by her. She
never tires of her unchanging realm because it is impossible for an artist in a
constant state of grace to become bored with infancy, something that occurs
to the perverted or aged; nor does she grow weary of her passion because this

only happens to the feeble-minded.

Let us attempt to describe the attitudes and gestures of these children of Norah Borges. They are created in that zone that is halfway between childhood and the realm of angels, the latter being their rightful place. At times these beings reflect the fear, which often becomes astonishment, of the creature fluctuating between the two bodily modes. They are angels that haven't finished falling to their feet or creatures that view the heavens in swift, fleeting flashes, between one prank and another, remaining as such in order to continue playing with balls or hoops. A willful clumsiness characterizes their walk and the way that they sit down or handle objects. Their gaze questions, with more foreignness than curiosity, the inflexible lining of the floor that injures them; their slightly stiff hands are already able to hold, but don't yet know how to seize. Real children have always given me the impression of being small animals of prey, dominating with more mastery and violence than the adult, wounding with a ferocious bite, and even a glance, possessing infinitely more impertinence than the rest of us. But the children of this Argentine must have been something like the archetype of the holy child or the child-poet. Our own Eduardo Barrios once considered writing a novel about the child-singer but then abandoned it. As far as we know, it is a topic that no one has covered, to my understanding, and one that would be worthwhile. Whoever decides to undertake its publication must examine the collection of children of Norah Borges in order for her miracle to be transmitted to the writer. Observing the hours without ever tiring of Saint John, Child of Donatello, I thought that the expression of marvelous tenderness could also be that of Petrarca or, if you prefer, of Musset.

A woman without children is simply not possible, and in such an isolated case it could never be Norah, who found herself in a barren condition. She then sought them until she found them; better yet: she conceived them with a pencil, which called to them like a whistle, and thus one finds them here, the multitude of little ones.

A particular Eastern story recounts the tale of a child who, after having been enclosed in a room for some time, is brought out into the light of day and asked what it is that he sees: "I see beauty." They confine him once again to the room and release him during the night, to which he replies: "I see ugliness," which is his view of the night. Norah has only seen the day, with those gorgeously soothing colors, those of waves, reddened skies, and tender flesh. May she be enclosed before the West becomes angered with the singular, inevitable word, "ugly."

As with all great painters, Norah Borges brings to her works her own repertoire of colors. Among those we could enumerate are some intense yet soothing blues, rosy pinks, and lemony yellows (how exasperatingly difficult to
name colors with exactness in Spanish). The choices made, here as with everything else, are the equivalent of confessions, and they transmit the pulsation
of temperament. Furthermore, in Norah Borges colors are dictated by the
angel of individuality, which is preferable to the angel by profession, in that
she has instinctively fled from dramatic, harsh, or offensive colors.

Elegance is not tragic, she would say, like Friar Juan de Fiesole, father of her
family. Nor is elegance sentimental, according to the brush strokes of certain
aspiring young artists. These colors eschew flatness as well as boldness. There
is simply an emphasis on color, with the objective of providing pleasure; never
clamouring, however, with offensive, brassy color, so as to not come across as
forced, and as such, unauthentic. The eyes of those who do not paint, that is
to say, we commoners, gaze with contentment at the drawings of Norah
Borges, which transmit to the viewers a vivid elation without leaving them in
a cloud of delirium amidst those who do not possess such a capacity.

I do not know the name that critics give to this style of painting with pure
light, which eliminates the excess with which color pervades the canvas.
Clean, luminous, crystal? The adjectives in this profession don't signify anything, and the art critic is often worse off than the literary critic, without ever
finding the adequate descriptive terms. They would say that the blessed
Angélico painted the genuine colors of the soul, separating them from the colors of everything material, and that in doing so he achieved his goal. Norah
never intended for her colors to wander so far that they appear intellectual or
esoteric; they remain steadfast in their willingness to paint that world, but in
its skin of an infant or in its ageless factions.

The task of rejuvenating such an ancient world would have cost many a
painter a great deal of wisdom, along with a certain degree of malice. Age has
not been a factor for Norah, nor has she needed to pull strings in order to pro-
cure fresh skin for these things; quite simply, she quietly brought to her work
that penetrating look which pierces holes in the shells of the creatures, rendering visible the innermost flesh.

Things are depicted exactly where they are: pleated with wrinkles and laden
with filth. There does not exist within her art a heroic transfiguration: it
occurs only when these things have within themselves an infinity of faces, and
the thrust of a resolute and noble gaze releases them from their shells, exposing their true countenance.

The colors of infancy on earth must be those of Norah Borges, and she brings them forth to shine, wresting them from a fate of misfortune. They had been distorted more than worn; they had been switched, not soiled, by the dreadful chemistry of time.

"The face is where the mask ends," says the Chinese actor that is accustomed to donning three or more, and here the faithful color sleeps in the concealed face.

Painters of children have had to abandon their age and maturity with respect to life, and they do so with resentment so that the child appears more youthful and innocent among and above them. But Norah's talent is more complete: she sits, or extends, or straightens the child on a beach, in a boat, on a hill, in a house, as one would with certain handsome baby animals. No part of the earth has aged for her, and her nativity, as opposed to Bethlehem, is that of the landscape, the geology, the air, and the animals. The marvelous caring in her eyes doesn't recognize ruin to the land so as not to offend it or to love it all the more.

We view and review prints and more prints, and the result will be this extraordinary Nativity, without an aged Joseph or graying kings or an adult Mary.

In reality, what one discovers so radically childlike, of bones near and far, is she herself, the painter of everything related to children; and that the world is not really as she depicts it, nor is it of importance to her. As always, it is a matter of the subjectively illusory planet rendered by an artist and placed into our hands for our pleasure.

Norah Borges lives inside of a joyful creature, as do the most integral creators: the Far East has already said this and known it forever. There are many illusions of happiness, but true joy, that which is similar to an intimate, heartfelt rose, the pleasure derived from experiencing the movements of bodily parts, both the visible and invisible, is only that which comes from one's own creation. In particular, it the joy of not having to depend excessively on others for support, and is not soiled by the sticky sweat from the work of others.

Therefore the face of Norah Borges must radiate knowing that we consider her our friend. She seems to spend her twenty-four hours under the intense and delicate rain of grace, underneath which she sleeps, walks, eats, and prays.

I enjoy in her work the offensive artist that makes it possible for those bad things to be called "naturalisms" or "realisms." She has established for herself a vigorous imagination; she creates with the most minimal of her body—at times with even less—affirmed by the truths of her subject: beach or field.

Why the need for more support, more attachment, more tolerance?

The real world is the face of the laggardly son left behind by Zola, who still craves to take "slices of life" and indulge to his heart's content. The reality of the tree or creatures is that they are fine where they are and haven't a need for society or friends to correct or better themselves. Our reality, which is that of the painter or the poet, is the most exact possible: spirited invention and absolute boldness.

A fable about Norah Borges could begin like this: "She was a girl that never advanced to another age. She drew only children, angels, waves and clouds, and all the other things that she did, in a style to accommodate these creations, were also childlike. They gave to her infancy, a peaceful kingdom in which to wander, and as she knew only of pureness and innocence, she never engaged in an intrusive relationship with other realms. From the walls of her home a throng of these creatures afforded her a gleeful society, a marvelous coexistence. Weightiness, awkwardness, shadows, confusion, she ran into all of them as we do, yet she quickly turned away to avoid them and to escape affliction and pain which she never experienced."

As I sit in the midst of an angelic gulf, I think that this is the home of the artist, the decorator of our schools, which is what she is without knowing it.

It is high time that the government and educators understand that the complete decoration of a school should not be based solely on the thoughts of our civil and military heroes or exclusively on the biblical allegories by which others poison the infantile mind. I have known them for years: the gallery of worthy individuals loathsome to children both initially and in the long run, and the sermon driven into the frieze only makes them painters of chrome. The natural decoration of the classrooms for our young children cannot be anything other than the immense and transparent frescos imagined by Norah Borges.

(February 1935)

Victoria Ocampo

In Victoria there must be many Victorias, as I personally know at least four. One is the stepdaughter of France, who knows them all—prayers, rounds and fairy tales—learned from the French governess who excluded the Creole dialect.

And to the side here of this one faithful to Sena and to Racine, there is a skillful, clever, sagacious one for whom Sena is not important for everything—for example, for the strong wind of adventure and for a certain freshness of institutions for their transformation into a large modern city, Parisian style. This Victoria makes her escape toward the canal, arrives on the other side and settles herself on the shore ten times over due to the gust of wind from the canal or from the Mediterranean; it is there, moreover, and only there that other gifts are received: a poetry less ingrained in the flesh and a prose more infused with music and, consequently, with elegance. And there is behind these two Victorias—whose dispositions favor foreign customs—behind these two intense whims which some attribute to vice and others to trivialities, a formidable Argentinean who, when she throws down the mirror into which she gazes at herself and becomes disfigured to her content, remains among us in her radical and most unusual Argentineness. She laughs at those of us who believed her facetiousness, as if to say, "What were you imagining? Did you really think, you incredible imbeciles, that one can have a pampa of this width and this vigor and a river like the Plata, and one can live with Martín Fierro napping at the foot of the hill, and not carry it in one's soul, just as one carries it in the body? Do you think that one walks with this lengthy stride of the greyhound and breathes with this neck of the llama and one delights in these interminable dunes, being from the Loire and dreaming of Piccadilly?"

From the moment that one discovers the deceit or the little white lie, seen in her face up close or in her walk or heard in her fit of anger so characteristically Spanish, all the rest of her black legend falls apart, falling upon us like an avalanche of sand.

And this Victoria is going to be the one who remains after the fissure, a tenacious and perfect block of absolute Argentineness hidden in the ivy or the European bougainvillea there in front of an exposed rock which appears to have never been excavated from its quarry. What remains is the grand woman of the La Plata River, and hereafter, no matter what they say, you will no longer see anything but this true one, configured in the image and likeness of her geography. No longer will they make you believe the myths of the Victorias of the clouded or deceitful mirrors.

This creole Victoria possesses all the gaiety and graceful ease that give distinction and dazzle to living, and nevertheless, she is also timid, perfect for what we regard as living, for what constitutes language (she designates as "self-expression"), in order to scatter her noble humanist essence upon paper. She seems to defend herself with her word, and her word would suffice as a mental document!

The distinguished literatures that she frequents, proficient in the classics and in contemporary texts, have given to her, with regard to her motive to write and to understand the literary text, a sort of superstitious respect and a fear similar to that which we women and children feel toward complicated machines, and that which we experience as well in the presence of an amassment of gold, as with the Spanish galleon...

Therefore I must explain, I, who often provoke bewilderment and am somewhat audacious within this noble profession, the lengthy journey and the scandalous delay realized by Victoria Ocampo until she became convinced of her very own treasure to offer and share with others, broad as the Paraná when it floods.

It wasn't long ago that she began to speculate as to all that she had, the wealth that she possessed, though not yet familiar with her passion nor her knowledge of everything in its entirety, from the sea to the mountains. This treasure is the result of an existence of blissful immersion and saturation with life itself. The wide eyes of the Mexican doe and of the woman that is our Victoria have seen the countryside in the morning, have unrolled the tapestries of one hundred cities or more. Her sharp ears, like those of the doe, are well familiar with the entire musical tree of this world, which has swayed its branches for her, even the most conflicting. Her noble intention has been to capture the essence of places and peoples of means, of the arts of living, which has made her compile a wealth of vital knowledge and an art of living, which she neither measures nor enumerates since she has not yet convinced herself totally of all that she has. Yet because she is doubtful that she has and holds them and because of her incredible reticence and a superstitious fear that almost seems like that of the Indian, she, while writing, has lived a senseless habit of affirming, of assisting, of lending. It is similar to the following: in the Chile of other generations, we little girls would play blindman's buff (in my Elqui Valley) but with a variant that some one of us invented. The blindfolded girl, whom we would release in the orchard, reckoning and making her way amid trunks of damson plum trees and woody grape vines, would suddenly hear, "The river! The river." When the "little hen" was an excessively timid little girl (I now say "imaginative"), she would stop short suddenly, arms up high, her face pallid or very red. She perceived the river, over there, just a step away...

The legend of Victoria undoubtedly will cause others to laugh at my comparison. It doesn't matter to me. Victoria Ocampo, in the business of writing, is the little timorous one from my Elqui Valley.

Her "phantasm" compelled her excessive reverence for the Masters and even a certain South American fetishism, which is the product of literary culture. From here one can comprehend the zigzag in her walk, her consultations with feigned little gods, the mistrust in their intentions, her reluctance to use her native language, because it was not taught to her as a child, etc.

I know very well that, pedagogically, this pyramid of superstitious scruples, which is equivalent to professional ethics, engenders laxity. I know that it is a noble sentiment and even the sign of refined lineage. However I also know fully well that to some South Americans, the excessive idolatry of Europe has wounded them like a paralysis, along with the mistrust of their spiritual brothers and of the potential of the Spanish language.

I am more than familiar with the gestures provoked by this creole affliction: it is a pursuit of the river of images; it is a mistrust of the language that surrounds one, even though it bubbles with life like the ceiba of your homeland; it is a passing of wheat from the fields through triple foreign sieves; it is an existence of squandering precious sensations and sights from quotidian reality only because they were created within a path marked by the scent of the sheep and cattle, which lept in our faces in a mountaintop village.

But this somber and wrought treasure was precisely what the noble Sarmiento gathered, accepted and worked. The reason for his success, however, was, among other things, due to his giving credit to his surroundings, his domestic affairs, and his writing about it, thereby conceding it value, beauty and dignity. This was foremost a matter of his preference.

From the left side, which is his younger son, he obtained his library, which never became for him a burdensome blanket; from the right, he took his Argentine Pampa or his Chilean mine or his school, striking his side at each step, as one carries a lover or a child to maintain a firm grip.

Victoria Ocampo began her work with three books of essays. The three of them are fine and not without exceptional chapters or passages. One of the unfortunate things that can occur to a writer is that he succeeds by walking along the branches of his being, and that in these he frolics a bit and becomes distracted—in the double sense of the word—thereby delaying his climb down the trunk of his being. It is very strange the fact that some individuals do not see themselves entirely, like the animal that observes itself in quiet water and can endure, linger and even remain for a time, remain outside of itself, and at times inside his lining, within his shell.

Victoria tarries considerably in those simple, naïve linings of the self; for example, in the clever ingeniousness of the genre that most seems hers naturally, the essay, the simple commentary on others. That seemed acceptable to her out of modesty, not presumption, as some might think; the arrogant ones are perhaps those of us who cast ourselves out into the wild ocean surf. Thus in her first book she tried to examine, explain, raise with difficulty the theme of women, from Francesca to Beatrice. The topic seemed sufficiently her own for her to express there profusely all that she possessed, that is to say, her magnificent femininity. But nothing of the sort; she did others, but not as much as she was able or should have done. It is impossible to touch even a finger of Dante without a bibliography the size of the cordillera throwing itself upon us, not only to overwhelm, but also to suffocate and drown. Victoria, who is audacious in life but not in her writing, acted not only reverentially, with tact, scruples and honor, but with veritable fear. The mountain of predecessors frightened her. Who was going to try to manage, let alone raze, she surely told herself, that continent of illustrious celluloid!

Afterward, chapbooks ensued—also out of timidity. Then two volumes of essays containing the chapbooks. But in the second volume of these "testimonies," at last, like the peeled sections of a fruit, the core of her vocation surfaces, along with her talent and capacity. In the one entitled "Emily Brontë" one encounters the rupture that enables the essence to be revealed. Victoria spent years of intimate treatment with two Englishwomen: Emily Brontë and

Virginia Wolff, years of not only investigating them in the European critical circles but also of keeping before her, like a secret chest or capsule difficult to force open and deaf at responding, the strange soul of Emily, of the novelist and the poet together.

The male genius always intoxicated her, but the female genius intrigued her. She was not content to merely read the biographies of Emily, her critics amounting to a legion; she insisted upon knowing the landscape of her investigation, of her impoverished imprint, at once supernatural and insignificant.

And Victoria, perhaps because it was a matter of women, being that she herself is very sensitive to the glories and miseries of our gender, to its humiliations, this time finally acquired some confidence. And high time it was! That splendid biography of Emily Brontë brought to us, her friends, a certain peculiar happiness: that of seeing her free herself from the two thousand ties formed by her Masters, both the great and the lesser ones, that bound her like a copious yet delicate mass of entangled whitish yarn wrapped around her.

Victoria Ocampo began to see in front of her an extensive and valuable land to be worked; she awoke upon contact with her own resources: she knew how to write about another's life...it was natural; she possesses a memory of people more laden and rich than grapefruit in December. She has had and has in abundance the lines, the pastes, the pulps, the juice of many grapes in order to render visible and make known all the species of humanity. The Museum of Wood in Sao Paulo contains no exhibits of illustrious and vulgar woods other than those documents rendered full of experience by Victoria Ocampo. The keyboard of the reed organ that belongs to the feminine gender is, in her, at a great distance, and she knows it key by key...

Why then had Victoria lived so many years making dates and examining the void (like some one else with regard to the Valley of Elqui)? Because of lack of self-confidence in herself, which we call wisdom, but which, in certain moral matters, is referred to as a waste of talent and an erroneous appraisal of the tools that one has at one's disposal for one's work.

Those of us friends who rejoiced at her "plunging into the subject," read a splendid biography welding, for the first time, her work with herself. I remember reading it in a sitting in which the legendary bookish Victoria known by all drops unemphatically a phrase, only one, regarding something: a book, a person, a fruit or a geographical place. These are drops of pure essence, but of that kind which emanates from the pine tree and from the myrrh, drops of that kind which slip ten meters from a vegetal heart before dripping upon the foot and falling into our hand.

Victoria is composed in conversation, never insulting, at times benevolent and more frequently admiring. The flow with which she expresses herself in books or in real life upon speaking seems magisterial to me because it renders visible the intimate fabric, even though that translucent fabric obscures comments from the Masters of the distant past.

It was, then, something of her conversation that finally, after such wavering, she threw onto paper, writing the essays. Not entirely, indeed; the mark still is traced for writing the "scholarly fears," but in her conversive mouth there is no superstitious apprehension.

One would have to determine how the French governess—whom she remembers with gratitude—taught her classics to our Victoria; and if it wasn't from that scholasticism that the compliant submission to the Masters came, and within that, the superstition toward the quote and the fatal attraction of South Americans to the formal perfection the French language gives or imposes because of its absolute reflection. Victoria, tremendously passionate, often appears somewhat concealed and distant in her structure, and that coldness, not of the hand but of the instrument, harms and disciplines somewhat the unfaithful daughter of the Spanish language.

Enamoured by the language that rubs elbows with the paternal Latin in terms of formal perfection, Victoria disregarded until recently the incompatible marriage made by an impassioned woman of the Spanish tongue expressing herself in French. It is a phenomenon similar to that of heresies: the infidel lives the tragedy of what he calls "divided love," and calls his confessors triumvirate of the spirit. In actuality, the renegade other continues living at our side like the mistress clinging to the lover; but the wife—or, if one likes, the Mother—is seated in the middle of life and in a leap, with a shout of joy, owner and madame of our voices, as this is of flesh, and as such this custom, tenacious and grave, orders and governs.

I always remember part of a conversation in which A. France sharply pointed out the risks of the Spanish writer who delivers himself to French. He affirmed more or less the following: that the two languages have contrary, even antagonistic natures. Perhaps one of the few classic writers who do not harm the Spanish people is Shakespeare. He almost attains the magnificent disorderly exuberance of our language in its audacious excess, in its euphoria and its passion. Racine perhaps is the opposite of Shakespeare. Dante is with us, chest abreast, as far as Catholicism and fire; but once again, the form, with its sizzling iron right on target and almost geometrical in its rigor, cannot compare with the blaze of Saint John and frenzy of Spanish, where the language is the people, the multitude.

For me, the linguistic tragedy of Victoria Ocampo resides in the fact that a dauntless character—I would even venture to call it a tumultuously passionate one—when kneaded and fashioned by a French education, by the fatality of instructesses and governesses, by sheer will arrives to the point of surrendering; it delivers itself to pedagogy as one of exalted rank and everything of an opposing language, at once attractive and adversarial; it has attained in us a nearly supernatural infliction because of its fatal consequences.

Quite happy she is; nonetheless, she is tremendously obstinate, like the wife who accepts the broken bond because, according to her moral standards, it seems to be fine or simply makes her happy for periods of time. Therefore I do not ask myself if the affected foreigner makes her truly happy, that is to say, the borrowed tongue. The topic comes and goes in her conversation, which is indicative of the particular conflict troubling her.

Victoria Ocampo, ample of body and wealthy in strength, endowed with vigor like the ceibo or the araucaria, Victoria impetuous in her willfulness, a character as pronounced as the rows of the cordillera, Victoria unrestrained in her judgments and familiar sayings. How do they arrive at agreement? How does she "get along"? How does she live in that language of crystals, anti-Rabelais, which French has become, according to Leon Daudet, who knows very well the anatomy of his language? And how can she accept the dichotomy of speaking in Spanish while passionately burning to write in a French as smooth as the beautifully varnished mahogany of the finest wood-carver? In what zone of the intellect and of the soul does she suffer her linguistic bigamy?

(February 1942)

EMILY BRONTË

THE FAMILY OF REVEREND BRONTË

Patrick Brontë, evangelical parson, lived the life of an impoverished stoic clergyman in the heaths of Haworth in Yorkshire. His companion, Maria Branwell, died leaving her husband, a man of daily Bible readings and weekly sermons, with six young children to raise in a desolate parsonage that bordered the cemetery, or, shall we say, coupled with the latter to form an extensive mass of stone.

From her own bed the dying woman would look out upon her burial place, anticipating in her body, as one would say, the unpleasant contact with the earth, and the girls saw their mother pass from her bed to the dampened ground as if passing from one bed to another. To have the village cemetery for a yard allowed them to reduce death to something commonplace, as these were strong and joyful children who jumped on top of graves without understanding the subtle connection between that place and their youthful legs. But the family of young Brontës, from one to eight years of age, much like the little mushrooms that grow in a similar manner, in clumps, in a humid place, would go away only to return, whilst the earth embraced them and came to possess them, will-o'-the-wisps who danced about the cemetery grounds.

The children's names were Mary, Elizabeth, Charlotte, Patrick, Emily and Anne, and for the Reverend Brontë there was not much difference among them, other than the young male, whom the father always distinguished from the others. The five small precious gems were, for Patrick Brontë, his very own flesh, and he felt obliged to cull and cleanse them in view of eternal salvation, paring from their education any pleasures that could become vices; only the young man was allowed to use his hands and his intelligence freely,

81

which he used entirely to his whim.

Each one had his "own" Bible and would extract from the enormous book whatever suited his or her fancy; the phrase "biblical education" did not refer to anything specific, because some individuals extract from the book the tasteless tonic of Solomon, others share with Isaiah his incitations and animated alleviations, and the uncompromising puritan seems to derive the most pleasure from the passages from Moses. The Reverend Brontë has whetted his bones with the pumice-stone that forms the Book of Numbers and the Book of the Commandments. His vegetarianism goes far beyond the list of foods enumerated by Moses as clean and unclean; the domestic discipline that he elects for his seven year old child reveals the flint knife incision made by those verses; and the will to obtain in six children six finished doublets surpasses the rigor of his own father, John Knox. In many ways, he seems like an orthodox Jew of any one historical time rather than an Englishman.

Given that the modern reader of biographies does not accept monstrosities, in an attempt to understand the Reverend Brontë, it is best to explain him in terms of this equation: an Irishman, plus a puritan, and to this add a widower, and the sum total of the three gives one the obsession of Patrick Brontë, single father of a family of six.

To assist with his young children, the widower invoked one of his sisters-in-law, who would not provide her nieces with much comfort, shall we say. Though not quite to the same extent as the Reverend Brontë, for her instruction meant sitting atop an iceberg as would a mother seal, and she was so mistrustful of warm affection, of any display of warm affection, that she completely stifled all expression of endearment among the siblings. She gave to them the best that the Victorian church had to offer: a certain nobility of customs, which in the girls will remain integral even in common surroundings, and a severity that, counterbalanced by the benevolence of Charlotte, Emily and Anne, will be, like the geometrical patterns in the delicate flesh of fruit, a joy to behold.

Their father would return home to be with the family only at mealtime and at night for the reading of the Bible, for he was needed by his children just as the midday is in need of the sun. When the Reverend Brontë took a respite from the Twelve Judges, he would make himself read, for the sake of his eldest daughter, the political debates in the newspapers, the six small children seated in front of him like stiff, proud penguins that hear but do not understand. With time the children became familiar with the names of all the "ases" of English politics, and together they discussed the Duke of Wellington and the

Minister of Canning before learning of the adventures of Gulliver and the craftiness of Tom Thumb.

One day the ideal storyteller for the children arrived in the form of the good maid, Tabitha Aylroyd, upon whose skirt one could play most perfectly with the little colored yarns of short stories, because Tabitha believed in the Spirits of Nature just as she did the bench upon which she sat. Thenceforth, and given that the Reverend Brontë did not slacken in his preoccupation with the Torys and the Whigs, the children jumbled together all the individuals with whom they were familiar, placing Wellington inside the voice of Gulliver or mixing the beard of the ogre with that of Holofernes, similarly thick.

The maid Tabby entered that house and lived in it like an enormous magnolia whose glorious scent cloaked that of the cemetery, and it seemed as if she had closed the windows on that side of the house. Thanks to her, perhaps, since there is nothing like a storyteller to inspire others to tell tales, Charlotte, Emily and Anne filled their notebooks with melodramatic narratives and verses. The little coins earned on Sunday were no longer spent on sweets but on the purchase of notebooks, and the Reverend Brontë ignored the heavy shower of booklets that rained over the slate slabs of the parsonage.

THE BOARDING HOUSE FOR POOR YOUNG GIRLS

Their aunt detected that something was not normal, and conversing with Brontë she advised that he place them in a boarding house for girls who were growing up without formal instruction, given that they spent the entire day shuffling between the kitchen and the bedroom.

The boarding of six children, when the father earns only three thousand francs, is virtually impossible; but the zeal of Reverend Brontë drove him to discover a boarding house that had been created for daughters of pastors, with an incredible pension of only three hundred francs yearly. And that is where Mary, Elizabeth, Charlotte, and Emily went to know that class of virtues contrived by the Protestant as well as the Catholic clientele: tight vigilance, abundant prayer until it grows wearisome through abuse, prime lodging in quarters, daily rations of penitence, abstinence on holidays, and a repertory of old maid schoolteachers who are unaccustomed to the shouting of children and see in them filthy little monkeys from Brazil that should quickly be transformed into correct British children.

After the time spent with Reverend Brontë and Aunt Branwell, the little motherless girls of Haworth truly deserved something better, and they found themselves in a situation far less satisfactory than before: their father prohibited that they eat meat, but the boarding house eliminated all foodstuff that was more expensive than porridge; they had to awaken needlessly at five in the morning to traverse the city, and the bedroom was freezing in the morning when they dressed, as it was at night when it was time to retire.

Charlotte and Emily left there after two years, taking with them both Mary and Elizabeth, who were deathly ill and whose little bodies had paid dearly while in that pedagogical slaughterhouse. In just a few months they saw their two little sisters pass from the bed to the cemetery, just as they had seen their mother. And the graveyard, with its earthen pillow tacked with sepuchral stones, took a giant step toward the interior of the house right before the eyes of the two eldest daughters.

In spite of everything, a home is simply a cheerful place and here the girls felt happy. They could now read classic and contemporary books to their hearts' content: Shakespeare, Milton and the delightful Chaucer, next to the fireplace, stopping intermittently wherever they wanted to share commentaries on the text. This feast of diverse readings, which was quite refreshing, did not hinder them from responding to the peal of the bell nor to pedagogical instruction which, when it did not bruise, impaled the subject.

Charlotte would continue her studies later on; Emily remained with the stimulation of her readings, to which Charlotte would add academic substance when she returned for vacations.

THE WIND OF THE HEATH

There is something else, thanks to God, that the parsonage and its adjacent corpse-sewn field border: the vast heath that extends as far as the eyes can see, and in springtime boasts its impoverished verdure, which for the girls is marvelous. The Brontë women will never come to know the favored lands in which verdure lingers without effort, as does the horizon, and the flowers are in the air even before they appear on the earth. The heath, which in lengthy stretches is rocky and abounds with briny moors, nourishes thickets of privation, and those stiff plants of barren soil from which grass grows thin and hardened. With all its deficiencies, the heath owes its spirit to a wind that seems more cast down from the heavens than blown in the sea due to its whip-like punishment and the shrieking of forces that so quickly descend.

The heath is no longer a barren, unhappy place when the wind arrives there. With its few shrubs and bushes, it executes its dance of medieval flagellation, and if one does not care to watch it, one can simply sit and listen to the polyphony of devils battling the archangels, the Michaels of heaven and the dragons of the earth, whose jousting arena could easily be the Yorkshire, Mongolian or Patagonian plains.

Little has been said of the wind, and more than in the poems that have tried to say something, the wind wanders in certain chapters that do not betray it, as in St. John's Apocalypse or in the circling of army tanks that can be heard in some of Walt Whitman's poems.

Maeterlinck, throughout the twelve pages of prophetic praise dedicated to Emily Brontë (*Wisdom and Destiny*), reflects upon and examines at length, searching to understand the origin of the tone of ancient tragedy in Brontë's work, the mountainous topography of a soul filled with abysms and thistly cliffs hitherto unseen anywhere else. It could be that the teacher who first instructed her was that supernatural spirit of the heath. What happens in the wind is something that we cannot comprehend by listening to it inattentively. Heard within the wind, wanting to free the land of its own weight, are voices haughty with pride or whipped with shame, confessions whose sincere tremolo surpasses our Rousseau's. Heard are the harsh utterances of hunger and vulgar greediness and the sound of gamblers' hands slapping bets upon the table. At times one hears, though less frequently, coming from a place where the victors are superior to us, severed soliloquies that only a divine ear can gather in pieces and compose tenderly. The sorrows and the joys of this world are expressed entirely by the wind, which traversing the cities recharges its engines and unleashes in the open countryside all that it lightly touched as it brushed against houses and towers. Emily would then weave these voices, capture these invisible prisoners, keeping them without knowing what they would become when she tumbled them onto a writing that they call somnambulent, which is really that of Shakespeare, her true father. The language of the heath delivered to her that compelling narrative which is called *Wuthering Heights*, and which makes one always question why the virgin girl of twenty five years should be designated confidante of this sort of tremendous secret of God and men.

Followed by her sheepdog, which the wind would often overpower in its rage, Emily would walk great distances every day, imbibing with her parched throat the wind's liquor, at times dry and other times mellow—a liquor more potent than the content of the wretched bottles.

The young girl knew no consolation other than that of these walks in the snow or upon the tender young grass. Apart from the friendship with her sister, Charlotte, a creature most worthy of noble friendships, she lived without these in order to lend credibility to her biographers. Love seems to have been for her like the wind in the heath: something beheld by the eyes but which never reaches the heart. Nor have the investigators found the romantic bourgeois love of a boyfriend in the village or that of a lover who pursued her for weeks. If, contrary to what we know about her, Emily Bronte did have a love, one would have to imagine a fleeting encounter on the plain with a total stranger who had been stopped momentarily by her green eyes and who had continued his journey with the wind at his back. The love poems of Emily Brontë are a disconcerting secret, like that of her very soul. Those who look for an explanation at all costs, the solution falling from wherever, have directed toward her brother Patrick those poems which they refuse to leave unexplained. What is certain is that the young girl who lived a secluded life, hopelessly endowed with talents, gave to Patrick Brontë a fraternal love that is only comprehensible to those blessed, impassioned sisters over the ages.

Absurdity, which is more common than we think, dictated that throughout Emily Brontë's life insignificant men would pass, insignificant men of straw and springs whom she could not, or refused to, clothe with the fabric of illusion. Whatever the impetus in her nature to spend on unbridled affection, she channeled into a type of brotherhood so profound that it resulted in ambiguity, with no reason other than that of being an act of perfection. Emily knew, as she knew almost everything, that a perfect brother is worth as much as a father and a friend together, and that his victory in this world is essentially our victory. Patrick deceived her with his small talents as a painter and a musician, which were really mediocre skills and illusions of talent. The young man possessed, in addition, that manly handsomeness which we women speculate must be appropriate trappings for triumph. Emily was punished for her only pride, as if her destiny of devastation also refused to allow her this humble form of happiness. The artist celebrated by the chorus of his sisters and the organist whom the people praised unknowingly ruined the palette and the organ to become a shameful Don Juan to the girls of Haworth and entered into the habit of drinking alcohol procured at the parties of the townspeople.

His sisters, especially Emily, experienced the daily humiliation of the family of the drunkard, a servitude like none other, waiting for their brother until daybreak to see if he returned home pompous or pounded to a pulp and then sleeping only after having put him to bed. Emily protected her puritan father from the breath of alcohol upon opening the door, and she guarded her sisters, both of them charitable but less merciful, from the shame of hearing their licentious sibling's demented soliloquy while she took off his shoes and hid his filthy clothes until the following day. One night she did not put him to bed herself and the drunkard tossed the covers over the candlestick, setting the room ablaze in just a matter of minutes. Emily did not call anyone; with her bare hands she smothered the flames in the blankets and the clothing; and in spite of balm, her hands were left bearing scars, which she attempted to hide by wearing blouses with longer sleeves. A little higher up her arm, the poor girl also covered up the scar from the bite of a rabid dog, to which she herself had applied the fiery stiletto. Once while washing her arms and touching the ugly scars from the animal and from the fire, she must have told herself what the superstitious peasant would say, and she must have said it with certainty: "When one becomes so unlucky that a rabid dog drinks ones blood and fire's tongue caresses one's body, it is a sign that, apart from God, the devil is trying to disarm him.

Brontë the father was familiar with his son's lifestyle, thanks to the scandal in the village and those nightly arrivals, which even the most compliant of doors allowed him to hear; to the life of his daughters he was incredibly ignorant, for the bells of vice ring louder than those of virtue. An inferior poet, in spite of grazing in the exceptional pastures of Isaiah, the Reverend Brontë would give his poems to Charlotte, Emily, and Anne, and he liked to hear himself recite them aloud, never suspecting that the child, Emily, who prepared his oatmeal porridge and cleaned his high-neck suit impeccably, would write in that loathsome house the sublime chapter entitled "The Death of Cathy," and without the idea ever occurring to him that during that time Charlotte was one of the best and most widely read English novelists. For some pastors, the Gospel causes them to become more sensitive, like the body of the gazelle, and they tremble, entirely conscious and attentive to this world; for others, the Bible casts them such great distances from the people that it encrusts them in a heaven, a sort of ceramic heaven, perfectly pure and perfectly deaf.

EMILY, NOBLE SERVANT AND MAGNIFICENT NOVELIST

When the housekeeper, Tabitha, broke one of her untiring legs while walking in the snow and the Reverend Brontë saw her crippled, he resolved to dismiss her because a table as needy as that belonging to his kitchen would not tolerate a mouth that did not pay the cost of its own food. The three girls begged on her behalf, defending in the loving old women the only precious pillar in that house of bats, but they were unable to convince him to listen. Little by little their father was becoming blind, a punishment to his eyes for having loved so little the light, their mother, which fortifies eyes while appearing to expend them. He should have called a substitute to the parsonage, handing over to her the part of the salary that was not divisible. The girls resolved, in the face of the calamity, to leave home in search of work, doing what never occurred to their poor, reckless brother. The natural profession of poor, dignified young females with a reserve of basic culture and honorable habits is that of a teacher, and they opted for the path most chosen by young English women of the middle class. When the time came to decide which of the girls would remain at home and take over the work of the invalid housekeeper, the one that requested the duty without hesitation and argued until she obtained it had to be Emily, naturally. Charlotte and Anne went away, and solitude seized complete control of the one who stayed behind with a moody father and a brother who was sent home from the tavern every evening. She accepted the companionship of work without any resistance whatsoever, assuming her role as errand-girl to the marketplace and as the resourceful cook who from a few coins had to extract a meal fit to be served to the substitute, who was a guest at the parsonage. She appeared as she always had, neither more embittered nor hardened by the change in circumstance; upon falling into this world she had been seated on a level of misfortune that cured her of awe, commanding her to exercise at one and the same time all of her judgment.

An alleviation in terms of the family's financial situation allowed Mr. Brontë to summon Charlotte, who upon leaving her job, returned home in search of Emily and departed with her to continue their studies in a Belgian school.

Residence in a foreign country would signify a great deal to Charlotte, who fell hopelessly in love in Begium, in true Brontë fashion, and produced from this hapless romance a winning novel; for Emily, this journey would bring about the benefit of her contact with German literature, which suited her nature more than the English literature of her upbringing.

After a year, and given that Mr. Brontë's money never completely fulfilled any of its intended purposes, the girls returned to Haworth.

This is a brilliant period of hope and open wings for Emily, the time of her full rapture with literary work. Sharing the table, the three sisters would sit together and write verses and novels. They wrote for the pleasure of expression, which those who live alone enjoy repeatedly more than others and which carries them toward a euphoria that the professional writer does not know; they also wrote because the literary adventure tempted the three naïve young girls in the same way that lottery tickets in a store window entice the poor.

"Why not? It has happened with others. A disastrous end to their reputation, and they can start their lives over again, still in their youth, when they have under their hands the material from which to cut the finest things."

Aunt Branwell died, leaving them some pounds or thereabouts of inheritance. Hidden from the Reverend Brontë, the girls printed a work in three volumes which they childishly signed with three pseudonyms between the lines. The booksellers gave them what they earned from the sale of two copies; the critics could not be bothered with the new poets of Yorkshire. Then the dauntless young women attempted a novel, remembering their endeavors during childhood. Emily wrote *Wuthering Heights* effortlessly in two months, as if in response to a dictate that fulfilled the command of the Spirit of the Heath through the borrowed hand of the Shakespearean virgin. Charlotte's novel initiated her literary success; Anne's novel did not raise a word of commentary, as weak in argument as the poor girl was in health. *Wuthering Heights*, somewhat difficult to swallow in the beginning, belonged to those kinds of unusual creation that require us to adapt our senses to it like the aquariums in which creatures of unfamiliar shapes, excessively heavy or quick, are moving about. The work merited a critic, to whom gratitude must be expressed for seeing something noteworthy, the antipathy that provokes a violent temper in the feeble. In the public of Victorian England, she raised a wave of fear and aversion toward "the brutal and perverse man from which such a creature came."

The editor sent money to Charlotte, and to Emily, also in Haworth, the dangerously absurd clippings from the newspapers. Emily read the articles with the same tranquility with which one day she removed her arm from the mouth of a dog with rabies. Her poems have revealed to us her fatalism, more determined than the devil, and she knew that her role in this world was that of the galley slave: to break and continue to break the hemp cord until the skin of one's hands is worn thin; but it surely must have disturbed her to contemplate the monstrous soul which had been attributed to her by a critic skilled in the search for characteristic traits and the marketing of personalities.

English critics learned with Emily Brontë, until they would come to forget it again, that often there exist somnambulant hands that write while restraining octopuses or jellyfish, and that they are as harmless as the munificent women who regale with the lovely roses of Elizabeth of Hungary.

There were two things that Emily loved in this world along with the brackish, barren plains of the heath: her brother and literary creation. From both of these came the slap of ridicule upon her Antigone-like face. If only she, who apparently knew herself, had understood that she belonged to that eminence of the glorious spiritual aristocracies that either enter through the main door of consideration within their time or tremble outside without even the slightest comprehension, which would result in the most certain of insults. Her literary name remained in the basement of English criticism until a week after her death, only to enter immediately into a limitless glory which her tongue did not barter for her, belated in giving and magnificent in the repentance at not having given it to her, in befittingly regal fashion.

Patrick's unbound licentiousness took little time in breaking down his body which, like his sisters', was destined for a short life. Drinking and womanizing in ten years made of this handsome boy a gaunt piece of flesh, and Emily received in her lap his body shaken by delirium tremens, which is the "dance of the Devil's ultimate prank," and with her pure eyes, which had lived upon the warmed terrace of an ardent chastity, she watched that flesh of her flesh distort itself like the predator animal stepped upon in a filthy and slow agony, endlessly deplorable and disgusting.

Her brother Patrick destroyed and without any will whatsoever to fight so that the despicable critics would see her true spirit and restore her name, Emily Brontë began "a life of two months," which assumed an incomprehensible posture of humble suicide, complete with the capacity to beget.

Maria Branwell's tuberculosis crept into her as well as into the others: an irritating cough; she continued to walk though the moor under the rainy, overcast skies or on days of delicate snowfall; deceitfully she received the medicines which she kept hidden without trying; she never complained of anything, nor did she even appear despondent, because the certainty of her misfortune was giving her an intoxication as savage as the wind.

The economic solution had arrived at the parsonage in the form of Charlotte's numerous publications, and she was of those exceptionally refined individuals who remain until the moment is served and who do not prolong their enigmatic glance for long after the conflict has been resolved.

Her slight and nervous body, similar to the brackish filaments of the heaths of Haworth, was laid to rest in the aforesaid domestic cemetery, whose earth knew well the Brontë flesh, lighter, finer, and more yielding than the others. The pestilent soil continued to gain entrance into the patio and into the interior of the ill-fated parsonage to which Patrick Brontë, the stubborn and insignificant young son of John Knox, was sent to be indoctrinated.

(November 1930)

Doña Carolina Nabuco

Racial Essences

I reveled in the reading of *A Sucessora*, the channel by which a women has delivered to me the imponderable aspects of her race. The Spanish frequently speak of the writers that carry within themselves the "essences of the Hispanic." You are, for me, the sublime conduit of an array of Brazilian "species," which I would have delayed in perceiving, gathering and assimilating.

I regard women as more imbued with the wisdom of life than ordinary men. But what astounds me every time that I read women's writing is that they do not place nor do they display in their writing all that they know. Perhaps they disdain their treasure, or they consider it valid only for their own lives, and they err in the neglect of this unmined wealth.

You have utilized your fortune—as a sincere woman, you could not have done anything else—and thus, like the first of your books which entered my being, it finds itself fraught with its dual experience, racial and feminine. It is a sweet key that opens the door onto the domain of Brazilian sagacity. A common error in Spanish America is the belief that Brazil constitutes merely a branch of Iberian culture, but I know that your Brazil, in relationship to Hispanic America, represents much more than the segment of a branch. It constitutes on its own a spiritual sphere.

Ignorant of all novelistic techniques and very conscious of my deficiencies, I am expressing here, most awkwardly, the pure delight, the absolute satisfaction with which I read your novel. This enchantment results from the pleasure always experienced by seeing and touching, in conversation, in acts or in books, the maturity of one's intellectual powers, and also by the affinity that the authentic expression of a woman evokes in another woman.

LANDSCAPE PAINTING

Thanks to you, I can now envision the ambience of Brazilian haciendas and of urban life and a vast quantity of rapid strokes of landscape that, for their precision, are worth far more than an expansive chapter of description.

A foreigner once told me that in your novel of the past century, the marvelous Brazilian landscape was absent or extremely insufficient. His comments were due to the fact that when he was here, he became enraptured with that and only that because his eyes were not those from within but rather those of an other, a foreigner. Whoever is born and raised here, however, has to live and inhabit its sky and its earth unequivocally, just as he lives his own body.

There is a certain magic, Doña Carolina, in the landscape that you sketched in ten lines and in your indirect manner of suggested characters, which is not the great vulgarity of vertical procedure nor that of the atomist of naturalism. It occurs to me that this grace of suggestion may also be feminine. Many writers still persist, in the jaded task of presenting their characters in the developmental process, to reveal and enumerate for us even the most insignificant details. How they fatigue and annoy us!

Illustrious individuals probably have defined already your style of narrative writing; I, a woman without knowledge of novelistic technique, only know to see in this certain consequences of the person within the work.

VERBAL DOMINION

Throughout A Sucessora a seamless command is enjoyed in terms of style, in the vision of life and in other unabashed circumstances. "Dominion" is what I call unpolished gold from her Portuguese, exempt of verbal explosives; "dominion," the classic naturalness in dealing with emotions without tarrying in them for excessive pleasure; "dominion," also the absence of reprimands and of theses from the past century, and now it returns like an epidemic. The dominion of which I speak is not the so-called "recognition of class," rather something evident yet impalpable for which Saint Frances de Sales would praise you like a temperance of the soul. The aristocrat habitually writes books without any refinement whatsoever and, by contrast, often appearing fraught with it are those of a Saint John of the Cross, son of a servant.

Few times has a writer either metaphorical or lyrical caused me such happiness. It seems to me that you are the novelist par excellence that creates only what is hers without resorting to collateral genres, in order to give the text more life or make it more convincing. Like you, equally permeated with human experience and equally clean of strange resources, the Spaniard Don Miguel de Unamuno wrote his novels, and you remind me of him in your racial permeation.

A RACIAL WRITING

Even though someday men may go so far as to abandon the endeavor of a true internationalism—because the experts are of a detestable falseness—even then the foreign reader will experience the same happiness as I in extracting from a narrative the virtues and the customs of a region. I have devoured and imbibed a solid Brazilianess and another subtle one in A *Sucessora,* say what you will, that it was never your intention to write a novel of customs and that there is nothing regional in your language.

In the handful of Brazilian attributes, touching each other like two roses, are a verbal discretion and pulchritude as wrought and consummate in our language as in French. One could say that the Portuguese people, upon receiving the Tropic as destiny, have imposed upon themselves a formula that spares them the dangers of a new dwelling. It seems that you have successfully expressed it: besides the heat of the sun, a greater obligation in proportion, and for all extension of territory, a sharper sobriety. This tacit vow has been fulfilled by the older Brazilians of the past, among them your illustrious father.

Your Chilean reader, who followed the opposite course, inasmuch as she acquired a tropicalness, what with her being a creature of cold lands, celebrates, nonetheless, the difficult Brazilian undertaking, which approximates a Christian heroism opposed to an anxious and invasive nature.

A RUINOUS ADVENTURE

When I had the honor of meeting you, Doña Carolina, A *Sucessora* and *Rebecca* were still quite the rage, and we conversed over the burning coals of the topic. I will never forget your tranquility in front of the pillage on which the rest of us commented with bitterness. "Misfortune, if that is what one may call it, has brought me one reward: the strengthening of self in order to continue in my profession more determined than before."

And it is because the writer, tempered in the reliable kiln of his trade, which is no trifle, possessing familiarity with fire, is prepared for this and other perils of this occupation, which departs from the confined flame of the soul and heads toward the rigors of the street and the plaza. They all more or less dedicate their work to Time as Shearing, who for not being an absolute man, stopped enduring the marketplace confusion.

What follows is an ancient adventure, filled to the point of overflowing, literary imitation that runs the gamut from simple influence to outright plagiarism. Critics often see it with the smile that produces an aquarium of abysmal fish, as weak as they are bizarre. Others consider the calamity of the copyist with the scientific indifference of one who studies phenomena that provoke a meteorite in the atmosphere. The excellent book appears and due to a physical law it survives the commotion and the outcry in the literary community. The completed work seems to develop substantial heat in its brief body (a mystic would say that the quality is radiance), and that animates its entire sphere. The rhetoricians call imitation enthusiasm, ennobling it with the classical epithet. The most prudent take it for pure naïveté, as there is no plagiarism that time does not keep watchful nor proclaim publicly. But everyone grants it a significance of lofty approval and of homage conversely. A creole of direct expression calls this the "applause of the Devil," the twisted praise or acclamation that is given with the left hand. You, on the other hand, wounded in the most sublime possession of all, which is the spiritual, only have commented that wrong compels you to good... All the more Christianity have those individuals who glance upon their spoils a look so elevated and so kind.

What a curious affair it is and always shall be this partnership of books and women! With what interest, at once passionate and anxious, the female English novelist will experiment with respect to your work! Isn't there a novel almost perfect here and doesn't it tempt you? The fortunate one will look toward the South like one who made the trip and took from some museum a particularly mysterious treasure that she regards as the most valuable object in her home. The champion of the "team" will never be able to forget your name; previously she would forget that of a foster sister. "She who prevailed," according to a verse of Lope, will desire, more than any other reader, to have before her a portrait of you and to read your biography.

Ultimately isn't this romance marvelous, in the face of the other, like the symmetry of leaves opposite one another on a branch?

A TRIUMPH FROM THE SOUTH

One must tell you about a clever triumph that benefits South America: your book has made a breach in North American and English literatures: the degree to which you reached that distant and unruly sensibility for us was such that *A Sucessora* was incorporated in a flawed manner.

Some South American novelists have been translated to English; others were appropriated by Hollywood, but the thundering triumph of *A Sucessora* has not previously occurred. The world is so outlandish that this Latin American victory arrives to us like the precious Paulist cloth turned toward the reverse side. But even so, what has happened is a triumph: the solid wall that separates the two American temperaments has been razed and crossed for the first time. The South pays for the success brought forth by your literary work with its own personal harm, but the Wall of China has been leveled, and what is important is this accomplishment. Great collective endeavors tend to have a somewhat picaresque beginning and depart from the outrage: allow the historical piracies to recount it.

Once again the answer that comes to us from yonder concerning Ibero-American creation will reach you, Doña Carolina, and not offensively, rather in a cunningly artful maneuvering.

A SUCESORA IN SPANISH
Your novel will be coming out very soon by Chilean publishers, in a twin language and it should be well received by you. My words are thus like a welcome of sorts that is given in a country to a face both known and admired throughout another meridional land, by a person somewhat errant yet faithful to her paths.

(July 1941)

LUISA LUISI

In a school in Río, Enrique Fabregal suddenly gave me the news: Luisa Luisi had died when I was traveling by sea, as one says heading for one's encounter; I remained dumbfounded, my thoughts abolished by the phrase announcing the death, which I already must have known, given the infinite times that they fired it at me directly in the chest. But the heart does not take to the catapult nor does the intellect become accustomed to the arrow. Upon passing by the crowd of children in the meeting room, I wanted to convey to them, with the naïveté of a child, the totality of my pain right then and there, in their very own house, and I asked them to pray with me for the Mother of the Stones, who spelled aloud the alphabet for other children, taught them the map of America as though it were an animate object, and sang in chorus with them the universal verses of poetry.

Luisa Luisi, much more for me than a female author friend of mine, was one of the spiritual forces of America. The death of a vital being, whose protection I often sought, as though she were a mighty hearth, left me stammering with the awkwardness of a child: "Is it true? But is it true?" I haven't wanted to acknowledge that from this day on, I'm much more impoverished and all the more so alone.

Nevertheless, I had left her quite sick in Montevideo and I had known for the past ten years that her body, that vigorous mast that contemplated the Atlantic and was seen passing through the park of Montevideo, was failing from her fights. But knowing all this did not alter my perception of her: there are so many hidden resistances, so many ineffable resources in humans, and particularly in her.

Luisa was an admirable poet, an illustrious professor and one of the great-

96

est literary critics of America. But she was far more than that and she exceeds each one of her given names. One must not dwell on one name or another to honor her and situate her within the small cupboard of classifications, as is done customarily with those who are merely critics or simply poets.

There was in Luisa a small kiln of racial temperament turned human passion, that is to say, applied to all the fundamental aspects of the being. She could have limited herself to poetry and served it in a continuous fashion, with the objective of leaving in her name a vast poetic work. She also could have severed herself from poetry, which is harmful in the teaching profession, and written about methodology, with an eye toward creating for herself a renowned pedagogical name. Or, quite simply, she could have been the biographer of Uruguayan literature, alongside her educator, Zum Felde, and given complete breadth to her enormous capacity to judge. For her, literary texts were transparent.

Refusing to adopt anything to the exclusivity of something else was her tremendously large heart, which she carried backward and forward in an effusive agitation from one earthly misfortune to another without establishing herself in any one desiccated kingdom; and she eliminated in her life the words "residence" and "rest."

Her engaging and enthusiastically warm disposition did her harm while benefiting everyone else. Each of us have been left with fragments of her labor in our hands, a study, an investigation, intelligent counsel, a profound poem of those which surpass the pitiful melodious poetry of the whistling blackbirds.

It would be a matter of recounting, convoking her friends, and thus we would understand the reality of that insanely productive life. Instead of commenting upon the three or four books of hers that we know, we would discover that she gave the yield of several writers to her progeny.

I want to share something about the chapter of her poetry. Popularity, which always is an affair of little, if any, relaxation, did not adopt for itself Luisa's poems. There was in them an intellectual inclination that people refuse to undertake; these were firm, acerbic berries that the multitude kept at a distance, preferring others more fruity and agreeable. At any rate it was inspirational that heroic poetry was applied by its author to her own inner life. The greatest American was Luisa Luisi, in her minutely careful attention to the intellectual task of these peoples. In her search for materials for an authentic knowledge of the Continent, her library did not lack a single Creole book that might be fundamental to her American culture. For her, the latter was regarded as an animate organism rather than as the bibliographic weight perceived by those professors who were stone-cutters of useless erudition.

Her apartment, which I see as I write, reminded me of one of the gorgeous bookstores that I know, all of it invitingly warm like the owner, without vice nor poverty of space, fair honeycomb of the great worker bee that died stockpiling wax and honey for the bitter present and a future that she was not to witness.

I went to that house in search of Luisa's contract, which was particularly dear to me, and to look for some practical books. She loved to help anyone who arrived at that studio house, also putting into this an intense passion to serve, which came to her from her Italian heritage and from her very kind country. Her conversation fascinated me, in literary matters, because of its order and clarity; I kept myself at her side to hear her speak with a resplendent intuition of the permanent virtues and of the ephemeral qualities of American and European works. All that one can know by experience and by instinct—a sea gull with respect to the winds and the colors of the sea—and all the knowledge that light can have of the life and death in the beings that she possesses, Luisa Luisi learned from universal literature, and her judgment always went beyond that which culture alone gives, becoming a vital operation. Because of the duality of her nature, that of science and of passion, of experience and of divination, there was in her a perfect critic, particularly a critic of poetry.

The phrase creative restlessness is the one that comes to my tongue as I recall her literary production. This constant fever produces in her the desire to better such an institution, or to defend some Uruguayan doctrine that she saw in danger, or to rehearse something that was lacking in that country, destined, according to her, for social perfection and nothing less than that by virtue of a democratic regime.

It is very probable that I, more than Uruguayans, know the warmth of her patriotism, and I consider myself blessed to be alive in order to give testimony on this matter, which is in need of clarification. Luisa believed in a specifically democratic mission for Uruguay in America, in a personal destiny that it would have toward this end and which it should never renounce. She consequently put her youthfulness to the difficult task of clearing the land, still a bit feudal, and of advancing incipient improvements. As she was prodigiously lucid, she saw that democracy, plain and simply, when served by a team of men of the highest order soon left behind its collection of reforms and ran the risk of losing its flavor and efficiency, like gnawed foods that become a formless mass. Then she entered socialism, in her own way, which was not the frigid mode of the Marxist technique but more similar to the style of the factories where codes govern machines, but very associated with fire. She read, discerned, and traveled mentally throughout the socialist countries and learned from them more than that attained by those who go to Europe to study and investigate, with enormous remuneration.

Luisa must have thought little after realizing that the material content of socialism was not so great so as to remain with it for the rest of her life. It resembled, according to her, the short-range veins that begin with a powder flash of brilliance and are exhausted within one hundred meters. Uruguay, with another team of leaders who also understood it, exhausted parliamentary socialism, almost with tragedy: such is the capacity to attain while burning the various stages, which that nation possesses, truly a political phenomena among all of our nations.

Then Luisa tasted the great temptation; she glanced toward the Northeast, in search of the famous Russian "Aurora Boreal," which was preached to the people like the twin of the Christian advent.

Luisa was fifty years old, but her pure life had maintained for her the strength of her youth. She slipped toward Communism, but always because of those weak dips of emotion, cherished by women, which ultimately inhibit the ability to scale back up the tragic cliffs of the Revolution; Luisa slipped down those Christian slopes of extreme piety called evangelical politics and which never succeed in becoming an ideology of perfect songs. I am relating what I know through Luisa and through my self, although I never have gone so far as to undertake the novel excursion through these lands which border the fiscal latifundium of Mr. Stalin.

And here my news darkens, and disconcerts me on account of the impreciseness of the facts. Did Luisa become an exemplary Marxist, that is to say, mature and consummate? She never confessed it to me nor did she deny it. She crossed that strange zone of the limits, as did Leon Blum or Waldo Frank, and she herself, because of her honesty, could not answer with a simple word.

Once, in Chile, crossing the Andean cordillera, I arrived at the famous place of the division of Argentine-Chilean waters, touching that magic place that they call a border. There was no such Andean backbone nor a separation of peaks. What I encountered instead was a gorgeous, capricious chaos of ascents and descents, and in the blindness of the immediate clouds, it appeared as an immense diffusion. Many times I have lived the same experience with ideological borders, above all with religious ones. But I have refused to remain there because of a stubborn will that makes everything vague disagree with me and makes me detest whatever craftiness there is in the cloud and in doctrines without delineated contours.

I treat this great deceased woman with the keen judgment that veneration commands. Nothing matters here such as the "until what point" nor the "when"; what matters is the "how." How extreme was Luisa's socialism in the year 1894?

I attempt to understand that she was one of the intellectuals and not one of the politicians. One of Michelets some fifty years ago, one of Romain Rollands later, which is to say, one of the French who never lets go of the pledges of national ideals and another Frenchman who has finished with a trip to Canosa to see the bourgeois Communist catastrophe of his country.

The last letter I received from Luisa more than authorizes me to express here what I am saying, the war already under way in the affliction she was carrying, and that has nothing to do with the Marxist jubilation that I see and hear all throughout America due to the life-threatening dangers in which liberal democracies find themselves.

Let us leave aside, though, at this hour of her warm body, the dispute and discussion that agitate the soul. Let the bourgeois of excessive action not become frightened by the memory of Luisa Luisi, nor let the ultraorthodox Stalinists bargain her away, because she did not celebrate the dark adventure of Finland, and let the believers not smell sulfur in the air upon hearing the name of the so-called agnostic. Listen, every last one of you, to what I have to say.

When again I met with Luisa Luisi, fifteen years later, she was bursting with good news. She now was a believer, she finally believed; she had allowed herself to be penetrated by certain oriental rays, useful for examining the enrichment of life through belief. I smiled upon finding a large photograph of Krishnamurti upon her desk, and as always we revealed to each other the truth, even the bitter aspects of it. I remember that I asked her:

> And why Krishnamurti and his modest method instead of the Uspanidas, which are the great ones? Why this kind of orange-flower water, if you have within your reach the classical Hindi, possessors of the wineskins of millennial elixir?

And with her unalterable mental clarity, she answered me:

> You, Gabriela, should be happy, because in the sensitive writ-

ing of Krishnamurti there are Christian influences, and from it I was able to move to your Gospels. The Uspanidas, so chaste, would carry me, by the hand, much farther away, and perhaps I would never return from the journey, even though you have come and gone.

Luisa was quite changed as a result of her reconciliation with religious matters; there had been a period of thirst in her spiritual life which had become quenched with those glorious dewdrops of meditation which refresh the burning and replenish the garden of the soul when it begins to become sparse.

No; nobody should withdraw homage to Luisa Luisi, a women of absolute eminence, cause of pride for that Eastern Band, Uruguay, whose disposition is composed of pure spirit and great dignity, in the most exact sense of the word "dignity."

The discussion around Luisa must end. The famous "Sun of the dead" serves to dissipate the opacity of blindness, and the mist of slight malice in our nations is exhaled constantly upon the individual whose superiority exasperates, because of the daily spur that is applied to common indolence.

The very death of Luisa expresses the ineffable love of the gods for her. She has departed before witnessing the shame extended over Europe, which was the Continent that formed her, and before her face turned red with the shame at which we are now having to look, in our own cheeks.

Perhaps the watchful God the Father has saved her from witnessing the insane creoles transport to America, with utmost diligence, the bloody-thirsty operation of the Old World. She will not see the sands of the South bloodied nor hear the fraudulent discourses with which demagogues from both fronts attempt to convince the innocent, overgrown population to then cast us downward toward the neat and pompous surrender of all that is ours: customs, institutions and the pleasure of living.

The fire of Europe, which walks with flaming tongues above the Atlantic tide, reddens eyes that sting with tears above the page I am writing at this very hour, when they should be crying only for the death of Luisa. She received the blessing of dying in time to depart whole and clean, before the division in which we are going to enter by the grace of Caribdis and Scilla and in which brothers will no longer want to recognize their shared mother, the America Rachael from whom we originate and who is our only obligation.

Guard us, grand vigilant one, sublime and watchful madam, and shower us with some of your broad intuitions, with the objective of impeding us. You are finally in the kingdom of Unity and already know, for all time, what we, inebriated with plurality, do not want to learn, headstrong and troubled by confusion.

You, sister, be for us now somewhat of a mother and make us look at each other and pause in silence for a moment before we throw ourselves into the struggle. Nothing more than for a moment, with our eyes placed upon another's in a fixed gaze and your name upon our lips. Let us do this, my friends, all of you from yonder, I from Brazil, let us do this for the sake of the love of Luisa Luisi.

(February, 1941)

Doña Blanca de los Ríos de la Lámperez

Small, prodigiously small, a third *menina*, a third elf, and a third fairy. (*Menina* is the childishness; the elf is the gracefulness; the fairy, magic.) When she was younger, she searched for books among the shelves of the lofty bookcase; later, she would pass weeks and months in the tyrannical rooms of historical libraries, inclined over one of those medieval tables, seeking consolation in Menéndez Pelayo. Still very small, having traversed the Castile of her passion, she then walked with the same watchfulness throughout the unbound geography of her America.

From the fairy she did not receive the game of playfulness; she brought a serious mind, driven like the thrust of the Spanish lance with respect to weighty matters of this world: historical, mystic, and political, but political in the style of Catherine of Siena.

On her head, which is not that of the elf but rather solid, two eyes of a blue that is delicate and piercing, in two successive blinks. A certain blue, which I call bluish, strikes the eye as ordinary; hers is entirely something else. Observing her I thought that she had procured the most perfect eyes of a mother, and that God had left her without a child. With this feature of blue she was able to look at the other Blanca from Castile, whom she very much resembles. Had it occurred to her to employ a pseudonym, that is the name she would have carried and without bending underneath its weight. It is all of Castile that fits, with more lineage upon one's shoulders than any one of the *infantas* or daughters of the King of Spain. She knows the country well, mystic to mystic, landscape to landscape, desolate or dusty: there is no other means of knowing it. She could sleepwalk, as in the proverb, without missing the door of the house of El Greco or that of the chilly little monastery of Saint

John of the Cross. There is no engineer nor constable who knows it any better.

She was the niece of a renowned historian of language, Don Amador de los Ríos, whose example must have put her in touch with his pleasure, the flesh and bones of the language; the daughter of an architect who restored with honor —it is the equivalent of saying with prudence—the Cathedral of León; the wife of another architect who has compressed in a marvelous synthesis the Christian architecture of Spain. Thus, Doña Blanca as a child and as a woman has moved among individuals that did well and expressed well. Pedro Prado would point out that the architects taught her to undertake constructions of her own and to see the aggregate of all things foreign.

The fact that she was self-educated saved her from wasting her feminine virtues on the benches of academia, dull and dry as varnish or goatskins. Something flawless, like creamy white milk, flowed through her thoughts at times.

According to Doña Emilia Pardo, only frail health, like that of Saint Liduvina, has prevented her on occasions from continuing that extensive work of hers, which I tend to liken to one of the Roman roads, direct, secure, and etched in stone, whitened by the Latin sun.

Spanish free will, so often negated, places testimony in her, just as it did with Cortés or Vasco Núñez. Isn't the shape of the peninsula that of a closed fist of Europe, a fist of Basque or Aragonese stubbornness, and for the same reason, entrepreneurial?

Her primary passion is that of peninsular Spanish, followed by the Spanish of the Americas; nothing beyond this is of interest to her.

Again and again she is classified as conservative, that is to say, privileged. Personally, I find the word somewhat offensive when used whimsically to place her in a hierarchy, their advantage always being their whim. If it is certain that she may have had her lineage cut from the cloth of Roldán, she lives, assists and labors as if the notion was excessive. I have not shocked hierarchies by speaking to her about that which is our very own: Argentina does not cover with its tremendous massiveness the wild palm tree of Costa Rica, nor does her friendship with the educated and oil-producing Mexico make her heedless of Chile. Instead of an air of privilege, in the French manner, I have seen in her and in many wealthy Americans genuine sorrow in response to the misfortune in Nicaragua and because of the alienation of Puerto Rico.

The dividing of Christ will be hers, if it is true that He divides: Lázaro, the popular one, equal to Nicodemus, patrician; José de Arimatea, senator, equal to Dimas in the compassion of the same Good Friday. Differences: the sterile fig tree and the others.

Yet unlike the racists, Doña Blanca has worked in opposition to Maurras, who would want to squeeze the Gallic core with pincers in order to defend it... She thinks that if the Spanish threw themselves onto the caravel, endangered themselves out on the open seas, and fell in the style of Ulysses onto the other shore, then there would be nothing else to do but to follow the bloody adventure with an assenting eye, from sword to sword, across the soil of America. The Spanish outcry has resounded disquietingly from the Río Grande to the Straits of Magellan, and there is nothing to do but seize it in Colombia as in Chile, acknowledging and accepting the natural differences that have taken hold from that place, and to refashion with them the Spanish tapestry, the extensive weavings of emigrated kindred.

Ten years of extraordinary life she devoted to the unsuccessful continuation of her journal, *Spanish Race*. Doña Blanca founded it after investigating her America, after having nipped at her customs and pried into her geography. When she already possessed the continent in her blood, she sat down to compose and was persuaded to write about the Iberian reality, nothing more than about the Iberian enterprise, in literature, history, science and economics.

The journal is something of ours in Spain, but ours as if it were the foundation of a Bolivian patio; even those that disregard it have in it their stone bench for work and for rest whenever they so desire.

Now that Hispanic-Americanism—I prefer the term Indo-Hispanicism—has become a pampered child in Madrid and departs from the palace reverenced by all, it is not difficult to turn the attention of authorities toward America. Thirty years ago it was entirely another matter: there was an abundance of arrogantly obstinate esparto grass to plough and even some small needles of animosity which had to be blunted for blood to not be drawn in the dialogue.

The bookcases of Doña Blanca, partitioned according to regions such as Argentine, Chilean, Mexican, etc., reveal how she spent some forty years without a trace of negligence, relentlessly researching and reading all that is ours. In the catalogue of her works, which recently appeared, I have counted ninety-seven articles and lectures that have been published. Converted to metaphor, this work is a dwelling of race; in terms of a scholarly text, its author would be called the "little mother of nations arbitrated against their will."

Another undertaking has taken many years of her life: the literary history of Spain, and within it, the corroboration of Tirso de Molina. Because of the refined precision of her work, Spanish critics know her better and regard her more highly. Our esteem is based upon this previous endeavor.

Doña Emilia Pardo would often comment on the curious case of a writer firmly resolved to reveal and restore the honor of a deceased individual. She saw herself compressed like the earth, surrounded by the figure of Tirso, immersed entirely in the topic out of absolute abandon, which Doña Blanca has scratched and excavated with intensity. Already the figure sculpted by Téllez appears more clearly in the Spanish light, cleansed of any unattractive biographical scars and in due proportion, the one that she, the loyal one, has desired. There had existed a tendency to fall into the habit of examining Tirso in the light of Lope. She believed always that they were equals and that the classification had been precipitous or malicious. She endeavored to prove her point and continues to convince the best of them, after a well documented dispute. A question of levels, something of vast importance for a scrupulous critic, and she is just that, a minutely cautious one, because of the zeal of the high standards of Spanish culture.

On Tirso's behalf she has spent no less than twenty-five years searching large books weighty with humidity or mothballs in her tracking of the fact that seemed distorted to her, and distorted it was. The search, more laborious than that of an insect for Fabré in the stony grounds of Crua, has often given her great pleasure, such as that of the discovery of the birth certificate of his friar. Fifty facts were placed in her biography by that little hand; that is to say, she reconstructed it all over again, shredding the deceitful one once and for all. The award given by the Spanish Academy, which reflects upon some essential piece and praises it, remains in good standing due to the epic attempt at rectification by this woman, who is neither more nor less than that of a nave in the "cathedral of the language."

Don Marcelino Menéndez Pelayo called her "well directed understanding," and others have mentioned—as always—her "male intellect," with the intention of flattering her. In a woman more than in a man are these varieties of patience, which some women expend in the plucking of eyebrows. It is the loyalty of a woman, this vindicating of the playwright who skillfully handled feminine intrigues; and the surrender of a woman, the feigning ignorance of one's individual work in order to continue that of Téllez in leagues of bibliographical adventure. It seems an utter absurdity to call those qualities, which are characteristically female, "manly" when we women can direct those toward our husbands and children just as readily and easily as toward the library or test-tubes. Here there was no infant to nurture or comb, and therefore the tender diligence became book after book.

After this case of Doña Blanca de los Ríos rectifying the lives of Father Gabriel Téllez, a writer can depend unfailingly and seriously upon a woman who defends the essence of a work: there already exists a precedent and a quite valid one.

Deposited in geological layers which include the purist, the bibliographer, and the journalist (in addition to the storyteller and the poet, about whom I do not have the time to comment), underneath and nurturing them all, appears the final one, which may well be the greatest: the grand dame of Spain.

A strong lineage of dignified nobility is associated with the first three mentioned. They say that for a writer, it is excessive, this business of having or not having ancestral background. It is not true, at least for a critic. There are enough among them that do injustice to their profession because they pitifully impugn others. As for this woman, Doña Blanca de los Ríos has been generous toward our humble America, which bears many unsightly scars on its body, all of which she knows very well. She straightened the crooked branch of the work of Tirso. Furthermore, she has been an equally invaluable commentator of the Saint who, because of the negligence of women, counts more males than females who understand her in the wheel of her praise.

It would be wise for a glass craftsman to observe her before she dies. One of these very days, we all know, they will request for a Spanish library a stained glass window with her features. There are already sufficient Felipes, counts, dukes, and the Méndez Núñez. Without fear of falling excessively, they can place in any official hall of books a Rosalía, a Doña Concepción, a Doña Blanca, a Sor Juana (the very Spanish Mexican nun). Then, dear artisans of glass, observe well the keen, gentle eye that I have mentioned and with an assiduous hand draw the figure of the bibliophile *menina* without missing a detail in the essence of her elegance.

(Paris, April 1929)

Note: A *menina* is a young lady who in childhood enters the service of the royal family.

VICTORIA KENT

Victoria Kent hails from Málaga, partly from English ancestors. The two bloodlines flow and express themselves in her character. From the Mediterranean she bears the human oils that Rome doused in each place in which it remained in the creation of a coexistence. Of Anglo-Saxon she possesses the understanding of worldly order through the organization of collective effort and individual lives.

Her formation was typical of the young girl who appeared promising in the secondary school of the provinces. After her undergraduate degree she went on to a specialized college in the capital which, like a fine furbisher, cuts, shapes, and polishes to a luster. She came from her Málaga fashioned by those ethereal and vigorous sculptors: light and waves. Castile perhaps has completed in her the work that they call the style or signature of the Spaniard. Victoria Kent renders a style visible in her life; and it is the Hispanic school of the future: an efficiency allied to refinement; an ancient profoundness infused with a purified modernity.

Tall, solid without excessive weight, with an Anglo-Saxon build and the face of a Latino, a solemn voice with an austere delivery that is becoming in the courtroom; her discourse, in neat blocks of thought, never wanders. Her person exhales a dignity devoid of arrogance. She is not the chest-erect type, which is how the Spanish designate haughtiness, even though her commanding authority drags women behind her toward social works. I would like to know the name in the physical sciences for the condition of weighty bodies that are not ecstatic but which rarely are agitated, and I also would like to know which materials, rather than being being neutral, are quite individualized and influence their fellow creatures and their opposites. The formula of Victoria Kent would fit between that pattern of physics and this other from industrial laboratories.

Now and then the human condition is blessed and falls to the hands in the form of a perfected example; one suddenly forgets the known failure of the many individuals who live at great lengths from the classical equation of man or woman. We hail that as the absolute triumph, after which one runs extensively, first exhausting oneself and finally becoming enraged. And several weeks are spent examining this individual with cheerful curiosity.

FEMINISM

In the professional organizations of women there are some females who attract more because of their character than because of their ideology. There are others to whom the acquired technique of the trade has hardened them as if overly exposed to inclement weather from the sea. And there is that more common class of feminism: that which fights pure sentimentality in a jousting list where tears are excessive. Among the mass of suffragists, it is rare that they enjoy the case of a plain and clean conscience. It seems that we women are scarcely-noted insinuations, slivers of a new moon of professional or political conscience. This requires a lengthy staircase of moral strata, and we will attain it in the future, but the process advances as slowly as our emancipations come swiftly. Unbalance disturbs and rightly so.

I would not trust myself to deliver the fate of my people to "the impetuous temperamental one" I have mentioned; nor would I accompany down the road for a lengthy stretch the Minerva-like woman, born of the brain of Jupiter and emptied of emotional entrails. As for the emotive ones, who instead of making music have undertaken the making of politics, these customarily become tiring with their garrulous ignorance. I would place, unquestionably so, any personal or organizational cause in the hands of a Victoria Kent, with her elevated conscience, as so many do fall within her family or her order.

POLITICS

She was elected to the Constitutional Assembly by voters who were familiar with the trajectory of her life, serviceable and straight as a Roman road, and there she participated actively, yet inconspicuously, in debates for two years. The seriousness of her character has driven her to oppose the rhetoric of the artful linguists, from the excessively elaborate to the outright deceitful. Wherever there is a practical industry upon which to place her hand, realiz-

109

ing the collective good, she takes her place. Unprepared in terms of the smooth skin which are our vanities, she will remain there, working without prominence, seated in the zone where the corrupt mind reflects less and fails to attract the novel or the changeable.

THE PENALIST

From the beginning, the Republic placed her in a position from which it could measure her energies and the nobleness of her penal culture: they handed over to her the office of the director of Spanish prisons.

She took with her that eternally dangerous material—dynamite for the faint of heart and for those who accept transgressions—which they designate with the discredited term "ideals." A true passion for justice made her follow the legal profession; then, her years as a practicing attorney, appearing daily in the jails—and what jails!—burdened her with experience. Unlike the customary theoretical criminalist, she felt called to realize in the charge everything that she had planned throughout her entire life: the reform of the penal system, neither more nor less.

She accomplished in fourteen months what is feasible to do in such a vast field of misfortune, warring daily with the worn armchair that is perverse habit. Her spade struck at the penitentiary system in the following ways: She increased food rations to the prisoners, as he who punishes should at least nurture. She doubled the provision of blankets, thinking that he who is quiet as a bench, freezes. She gave an order that astonished the authorities, that of gathering up the chains and screens in the punishment cells. This information sends an unspeakable shiver: she ordered the melting of worthless objects to take from them the iron that was needed for the monument to Concepción Arenal. She moved the bathrooms and the showers to new prison buildings. She eliminated entirely the jails which existed in an ineffable jumble with neighborhoods and schools in many places.

HEIRESS OF CONCEPCIÓN ARENAL

The work that probably gave to her infinite pleasure was the construction of the new Women's Penitentiary in Madrid.

Victoria Kent has told the journalist, Angel Lázaro, that throughout her life she nurtured the idea of this creation and that of attaining the position of general director of prisons. She told herself, just as she told the other that resides in all of us women, "Now I am going to construct the Women's Prison." She relates how she requested of the architect: "A lot of light, as much light as possible. A house like that in which one would want to live. Light streaming in from all sides. Six patios. Six terraces and a magnificent general platform." The love of play, cleanliness and clarity was not limited to the offices: a marvel to behold in the new jail, for example, was the magnificent kitchen. Forty-five bathrooms for the hapless clientele. Seventy-five single bedrooms, a large infirmary, a lovely assembly room, workshops well supplied for manual labor, the library, which is their daily escape to the outside world, and the blessed apartment for delinquent mothers who must raise their children (Have judges given thorough consideration to the concept of the incarcerated mother who nurtures and in that which she nurtures?)

Missing in the new prison are the "punishment cells"; they have been replaced with some solitary confinement cells for the rebellious recluses, and within them, the only penalty is the separation from other women. Victoria Kent has said that when a women enters that jail, she will experience a moral shock from the moment that she first steps inside the building, and that house will gently motivate the desired crisis of her conscience.

Situated in the Madrid neighborhood of Ventas, this white house serves as shelter for delinquent women. Its architecture boasts the dignity of things made for extensive social service; the geometrical simplicity that has escaped baroque excess attests to the judicial modes of the period, neither overly sentimental nor overwhelming. Victoria Kent must have experienced a profound satisfaction observing the dream of midlife fashioned out of stone and such an appeasing accomplishment. For the next three centuries, the female delinquents of Spain will live, thanks to her, beneath those roofs of clemency and behind those doors which, rather than cutting them off, afford them increased communication with the world. Saint Concepción Arenal could not attain in her time this completion of her solemn endeavor. She left her books in the same fashion that one leaves leavening, and in chemistry, just as in literature, yeast either explodes or causes the flour to rise, however heavy it is. After forty years, better late than never, Saint Concepción Arenal, a Galician, won her battle because of the arm lent to her by a women who swallowed her doctrine in a secret eucharist. "This is my blood," says each essential book to her tried reader. If such hosts are swallowed in adolescence, their effects are even greater upon us, and Victoria Kent is a case of those heroic adolescents who foretell and fulfill immense wisdoms.

When they told her that the task of penal reform corresponded to a male and not to a woman, she was able to answer that manly hands had managed the problem without removing it from its wallowing in cruelty and neglect.

When they upbraided her for what they termed "an anarchization of service," she was able to elucidate, describing for them what she had found, and to contrast the precious liberty she brought to the satanic anarchy found upon her arrival.

She said: "Either we believe that our function serves to modify the delinquent or we do not believe it. In the case of not having this faith, all the dungeons and the entire repertory of punishments will be too few. If we have that faith, however, one must give to humans the humane treatment that they deserve, not that of a wild beast."

These are concepts of the very logical mind that she possesses, even when the doctrinal elevation of them makes her appear to the country bumpkins like a woman of tearful utopias.

IDEOLOGY

The beliefs and political conduct of Victoria Kent are resolved in the angle formed by a passionate democracy that admits socialism and by a plan of realization that softens, by means of an intense culture, the realization of that excellent democracy. On this, as on other points, she walks with the team of Spanish female intellectuals. Her spirit of solidarity appears to be perhaps one of her most noble Saxon attributes: she prudently selects the group of individuals with whom to blend and whom she will not abandon in spite of minor disagreements in the past or in the future.

Admirable, moreover, is her judgment in Parliament and Congress; one could extract from her discourses a small anthology of social thought and political tactic, which would rightfully be designated "Breviary of Feminist Political Wisdom for Use by Latina Women."

What is to be esteemed in the political literature of Victoria Kent is the absence of virtually all forms of demagogy. Modesty is a scarcity among the political breed, whose duty is the beating of the multitudes as if they were the whites of eggs; modesty of the leader of stature is a delicacy doubled by the feminine condition. We do not know the ease with which the feminists fall face down on the demagogy, as a result of our passionate earthquakes and our appetites for immediate success.

Some of the female readers perhaps would like to extract, wrongly so, from this separate paragraph the conclusion that Victoria Kent is a delegate of the center-right, center-heavy or center-comfortable, and they are mistaken, because Victoria Kent is a women of the left and of a resplendent doctrinarianism due to her stubborn resoluteness. It is probable that in a nation of attained social justice, she would not found with her friends a radical social-ist party. But in the Spain that has yet to define the lines, as wide as itself, of the well-being of the worker and the farmer, neither Victoria Kent nor another individual of her integrity could elect a path other than that of social evolu-tion at a forced pace. The disorganization of the towns called Hispanic strikes her mentality with an iron whip; the hunger of Castile and Andalucía punish her senses when she walks over the chest or the extremities of the Peninsula.

FEMININE SUFFRAGE

Victoria Kent opposed in the Constitutional Assembly women's right to vote, bringing upon herself the hostility of the Spanish suffragist groups and a veritable explosion of the most ardent foreign feminisms. A woman, and moreover a delegate, wanted to deny the vote to her sisters.

She did not deny, nor even argue the right to vote for women. A mind as scrupulous as hers cannot nurture the concept of an eternal electorate of men. A woman that has realized the Dantean journey throughout the infernos of this world, which are called neglected proletariat childhood and rural child-hood, and which are called, furthermore, judicial problems and feminine jobs paid with the salary of hunger, has to think in terms of the creation of another rationality within the entire State, a need that will be filled by only that extra-ordinary woman who brings to the legislature untarnished hands and an unre-lenting conscience.

Out of complete loyalty to herself and to women in general, she possessed in this trance "eyes to see and ears to hear." She was all too familiar with the ignorance of the voting female population and asked the courts for an extend-ed intermission for the preparation of the female electorate. Victoria Kent resisted the lightheadedness of abundant wine or black coffee, which is the Saxon or Latin suffragist demagogy; she knows that it is not merely a question of we women voting but rather that we not arrive to that same field of uni-versal suffrage and duplicate the terrible horror of uneducated male vote. To accomplish the goals with the best civic talents and to, as far as possible, carry a rectifying formula of suffrage in general was her sagacious intention. The mere attainment of the vote and the satisfaction of vanity of her sex must have seemed like frivolous childishness. She has fashioned Cassandra against all the hearty enthusiasm of her nature, which carries her to an effortless manners of coexistence in the home as well as in the congressional assembly. Spanish women, for the most part, voted against the Republic which gave to them the vote, and this phrase already has been coined and carries with it an alarming reality.

A special kind of public opinion without incriminating contours, which is typically Spanish, perhaps will emerge from this voting assembly of women, which still does not know what it wants nor to where it is going. Nor, on the other hand, are these Spanish women voters a phenomenon of foolish ignorance or, even less, of Machiavelism. Quite simply, they were carried away without stopping to engage in a serious political function.

A PHRASE

I have found in one of her speeches, as if lost, a phrase of Victoria Kent, that flash of lightning that illumines the dark zone of the soul, and thanks to which often an entire individual is attracted. She speaks of the moral supports on which she counts for her battle and which arrive to her daily in the mail, and she adds, "One never forgets when a man or men disgraces us by calling us mother." This line of such of enormous beauty, which might have been elucidated by Don Miguel de Unamuno, brought to light a genre of motherhood the world would begin to know: the motherhood of the female director of prisons and of hospitals, or of the directors of daycare centers, which runs from the lifeless gray of weak functionalism, a pathetic piety, or a vertiginous mysticism.

DOING AND UNDOING

The reformist exhilaration of the first Parliament passed and there came a visual change that an optician would know how to describe. The proportions of the task about to be realized diminished; the Republic suddenly spoke in a constabular tongue as exciting as lukewarm diapers and artfully deceptive. Victoria Kent refused to acknowledge the Spanish Republic's reversal, and refused to make concessions, passionately working on behalf of its reform. She had to either leave, abandoning the molds to more compliant hands, or to stay, breaking them like pottery that disintegrates in the oven.

The time will come, or it will not, to resume the saintly task of the men's recreational prison, and quite unlike those who forsake themselves, she will be able to return, her plan intact, without damage or breakage, to continue it along the point and line at which it was interrupted.

Meanwhile, and for however long the interlude may last, she gives to those of us who observe her, at close range or from a distance, the luxuriant spectacle—Virtue lavishes upon certain individuals a veritable luxury—of an apostolic life, as direct in her approach as she is exalted in rigor.

(May, 1936)

CARMEN CONDE

I met my dear Carmen Conde two years ago. Her little book of poems, *Brocal*, had followed me halfway around the world, and it finally reached me on the Ligurian coast.

I began to leaf through it with great suspicion: it was a collection of poems in prose, and the genre, which I had also cultivated, had become very dubious. Generally we women, perhaps out of laziness, compose poetry in verse, which is the conventional norm. Characteristically we are a group of souls given to fluctuations between the poetic and the prosaic, similar to a fish between thin and thick waters that, without strong fins or gills, incapable of navigating in the pure poetic zone and at the same time lacking sufficient capacity to create beautiful prose, which is also difficult. A genre for the uninhibited and the flexible.

Yet in these matters of generalizations, a hand always jumps to cover our emboldened mouths, insisting that we judge each case individually. This time the refraining hand was that of Carmen Conde and the poems in *Brocal*. They were excellent, giving the assurance of a first-rate poetic temperament and opening a period of anticipation for whatever would follow.

I have remained hopeful, and it has not failed me. After having wandered about Europe and America, in the latter stumbling upon my "enemy," the poem in faulty prose, I had scarcely arrived in Spain when it fell upon my lap, like a dove that already knows her nesting place, this second book of Carmen Conde.

It was brought to me by its owner, and she herself read it to me, a pleasure that I rarely experience.

Carmen Conde is very young for the sound literary inclination that has

115

awakened in her. She is twenty-six, but she appears older, which means that hers has not been an easy life. One could also say what the Mexican Palma Guillén often repeats to me, soothing my face fatigued with French and making light of its resemblance to the California apple of the Yankee: "The soul protects the body from inordinate use, Gabriela; and excessive extravagance can facilitate the absence of the soul from the body."

Carmen Conde brings to me her own guest, the bundle of her works, and the presence of the child that she is carrying within, which envelops us with tenderness. As in a ballad, her child arrives in this cruel world wrapped in the first sash of poems about childhood. A fool would say that she brings it along with the book under her arm. It is better than that; she has worked at mothering throughout her months of marvelous lodging of the infant, and it has made her venture back to her childhood with the objective of experiencing and understanding the child better when it does appear. Lovely borer of memory this small hidden package of a creature who makes Carmen Conde play her juvenile games and skip anew in childish leaps and bounds.

Carmen Conde is married to a poet: Antonio Oliver Belmés. Both received their formation in the popular school of eastern Cartagena, and they work there with the dual passion of teachers and poets. This marriage of pedagogy and poetry, which professionals so often do not accept nor consider valid, I know is one of the very best alliances and one of the most effective. Poetry means, among many other things, a sustained level of incited passion, and pedagogy suffers from such aridness, so many barren spots of drought that upon crossing them from day to day, the unfortunate little ones long for the water of life, the blessed water that nurtures while playing, childlike; water that while it produces sulphates also creates clouds.

The pedagogy of the flatness of silica or of dry marl, which is the most common, achieves something other than saddening spirits: it coarsens them, cracks them, and ultimately kills them. There are already two individuals, Unamuno and Papini, among Latins, who have gone above pedagogy to say that it is doing terrible things—or nothing at all.

Carmen Conde, naturally, has not passed through conventional schools nor through institutes of higher learning. Some might say that this is the reason that she has salvaged her feelings without harm, pure and entirely hers; and that she knows how to see when she looks and how to understand when she listens. It must be true: constant pureness of the senses denounces in her a person with whom pedagogies, with their orderly discipline and their promising lands replaced by breathless maps, did not intervene.

The book is called, with a name of total elegance, *Joys*, and even though it evokes many painful stings, it is resolved in a joyful fashion. To see well, to hear well, and to touch well, are joys. It is subtitled "Poems of Children, Roses, Animals, Machines and Winds," and the pleasant litany of themes promises diversion that will be fulfilled to perfection.

There is a repertory of children, of clients of scholastic benches who are not impaled upon the bench, as is customary. They are there, in the penitence of school, yet they also walk freely, living in God's graces, which is, in eastern lands, something better than a "God's chosen." The best portraits, in my estimation, are "Gloría Hernández," "María Vega," "Freja," "Javiva," "The Deceased Jewish Woman." The exotic names do not correspond to foreign terms composed in the style of Pierre Loti. "Freja" and "Javiva" are Moroccan-Spanish women with whom Carmen played as a child in her infancy in Melilla.

Carmen Conde has undertaken the inventory of images from her childhood, of those not repressed, and she proves herself to be a marvelous recorder and delightful narrator. Between memory and writing, rhetoric generally does not meddle.

I love her and celebrate in her the tenderness in remembering. She loved those little girls from Melilla with whom she interacted at school, in the streets, and in the garden, and she treats them with a kind tenderness, as if they were the best of kin, which is true of one's girlfriends from childhood.

But what is remarkable is not so much that she loves them, but that she knows how to express that in those swift portraits so masterfully executed, with exactness that is never excessive. How she became so accomplished in this art of handling children skillfully with both care and wisdom, I do not know. She has given herself to an instinct she possesses, in part pictorial, in part lyrical; a disposition more joyous than that which we know of her, of dreamer and storyteller. The artist in this kingdom appears complete. At a glance the resemblances are read and more are requested; other Moors, other Jewish women, other children from Cabo de Palos. They began to live for us, these children beckoned by her whistle, and they came, and I almost set a place for them in my room so they would stay with me...

We need, however, to clarify that she has not created this mosaic of children according to today's models, in artful embellishments. The twenty-six year old Carmen Conde presents herself to us as a very perceptive woman, weighted with experience. Quintessentially Spanish in this aspect, she brings to our lips immediately the adjective that we most esteem in praise: compassionate. Her portraits, unlike the chalk or charcoal drawing of the clever sketch artist, are replete with humanity and fill us with warmth down to our fingertips.

Animation, tenderness and joy come together at once in these pieces which we would not want to call silhouettes, because, like Japanese drawings, they are multidimensional.

I skip this section, from which I would not willingly leave, to address another text, *Insomnias*, about which I have hardly said a word.

Someone, I cannot recall who, once said that "childhood, quite to the contrary of what is declared, burdens one with so many anguishes, fears, terrors, and enslavements that among the different ages of life, it surely must be the worst and that which one would not want to relive." I believe that there is some truth to this, but I cannot go quite so far. In childhood, with the little pulp of the plum and the rigorous imagination, the greatest fears exist alongside the most tender joys.

Carmen Conde, in this part of her book, returns to me some of my own evenings, revived; some nights of terror which I had long since forgotten.

These are admirable, stupendous, these *Insomnias*. Whoever knows how to evoke them as though they had experienced them is a remarkable truthteller and the best children's writer among us. Whoever restores with that freshness of recent weeks those sensations the rest of us keep buried and silent possesses a memory that God protects and an art that God allows to prosper in our lands.

Nights of childhood both marvelous and awe inspiring. The inviting imagination, those fantasies larger than life and those very small, are inserted with words from her friend, Shakespeare, and from Dante, her grandfather, without relying upon a confusing proliferation of forms, the interweaving of realities and absurdities, or mythologies more intoxicating than those that they already know by five and ten years of age.

Carmen Conde has uncovered a source to which we had been blind: the dreams of childhood. Flourishing profusely, perhaps excessively so, is the other fountain of Freud, that of adult dreams, lewd, provocative and repulsive. Carmen's formula, of which some might well avail themselves, is magnificent and will give endless dividends if it is followed.

Carmen loves the wind. She loved it as a chid and will always love it. It is the Holy Spirit of the land, greater than fire; but we know that and we say it as adults. Children know that it is the big child of this world, the one-stringed *tarambana*, that can do more than any other musical instrument; the worst prankster is he who corrects what they were wrongly taught in school; he who sets them free up and down the street or along the seashore to do as he pleases, which is consonant with the wishes of a child.

"The Wind in School" is the first composition that we find. "The Empty School" reminds us, without imitation, of the Andersen story, and provokes in us, the readers, the same process caused by *Insomnias*: we fling our memories headlong into the skirts of childhood.

I believe that there is no greater gift for which a writer can be thanked than that of tearing away for us all that we have kept veiled from view and allowing us to rediscover another world, lost within the folds of memory.

One would have to continue enumerating, examining and enjoying anew each poem, one by one. Many readers undoubtedly will disentangle the poetic threads and select better than I could those in which childhood occupies more space; that is to say: man is rich because whether expansive or sickly, childhood enriches us, whether we are wealthy or poor, for all of our lives.

The book is more precisely *about* children than *for* children, even though the reading goes directly to them, which they will thoroughly enjoy and understand. This *about* rather than *for* is quite all right. When we deliberately do things *for* them (and I am guilty of this sin), the results are often disastrous.

Several novelties of language are noted. This is the natural inclination of a master of language. She does with it as she pleases.

Carmen's feelings reveal themselves, selected and precise, and in her language of forty years we will find both matured and multiplied the beautiful inventions and polished audacities that exist here in the book of thirty-something.

We laud metaphor virtually everywhere as a marvelous key that unlocks a trove of treasures, and we hail fantasy, our queen and grand dame, without which nobody is anything in this business of writing.

But above them, or within them, we celebrate the perfect expression of emotions; those of night, those of silence or of fear; those of marine or fluvial waters; of air and of countless things. This is the work of a tremendously captivating individual, exceedingly feminine; in other words, that of a transparent, reliable layering that receives and responds.

How gracefully a woman moves about in her domain! Domain here translates to a cluster of children and memories of childhood, both of which are divinely served in these poems.

It occurs to me at times that it is indeed true what they have say about us women, with the intention of offending us and yet without offending: we are children.

That may be so, but there are some children far more conscious than others; some children more sensitive and capable of feeling deeply, more alert, that we may have in this world a certain command which has never been expressed or even specified.

We women, Carmen, may be destined—and underline well the word *destined* because it would be a complete destiny—to conserve, to supervise and to direct the childhood of men. The currents of freshness and naïveté that originate in their childhoods and then afterward, very soon afterward, become mired, cease altogether, or merely parch in their hearts.

(Madrid, September, 1933)

MARÍA MONVEL

The best poet in Chile, perhaps more than that: one of the great poets of our America, next to Alfonsina Storni, because of the richness of her character, and next to Juana, because of her spontaneity.

I began by admiring her and have ended up loving her. This estimation of mine was a result of her unmistakable artistic integrity. Effortless verses that surpass the cup filled with sentiment, effortless because of their plenitude. Emotion is never invented (something all too common among women). Her stanzas are exquisite expressions, possessing the exuberance of the green channels of Chile. Torture finds itself in María Monvel's spirit, but the word knows neither confusion nor hapless twisting. I said that her character was rich as that of Alfonsina. Indeed, all the human themes are there: the earth, the landscape, love, even coquetry, maternity, and playfulness. On occasions she seems a mature woman, and at other times, one watches her play like a child in frivolous matters. In truth, she possesses maturity, because pain advanced her life beyond its years; but she has not been poisoned by sorrow or bitterness, as I have been. She has watched over her heart, she has removed her eyes in time from the dark cave filled with with corpulent bats of sadness and raised them to the green meadow, to the sublime air. Her companion arrived in time to save her, and now she walks along a golden beach with a happy face against the wind, full of interior elegance, an elegance that comes from flexibility of spirit. Free from hierarchy. Distant from the Scribe and from the Egyptian Isis, for the good fortune of her enduring verses.

She is not a mystic, yet she is religious. She accepts faith like a muse of the many that visit her.

She is less known than she deserves to be; she is, I repeat, among the great

121

felicitous artisans of Spanish verse. To publish it is like adding a soft hill to the landscape of language; adding a refined accent to endearing words. In America, the finest have recognized her; in Spain the finest undoubtedly will celebrate her.

I said that I began esteeming her and have ended up loving her; she has a painful past that has made me see her most gentle disposition and to caress her with a pious hand. Piety is love; as there is no other true piety.

Now she lives the golden midday of felicity; now her verse can have the effortless and extended flight of the Chilean seagull, of the bird of silk and salt.

Graceful and serene young woman, proprietor of a poetry made to her likeness, let us commend her, let us give her admiring friendship and absolute praise. She is one of us.

(1935)

LAURA RODIG

At seventeen years of age, Chilean sculptor Laura Rodig was awarded the second place medal in an official juried exhibition, which others only attain at a more advanced stage in their careers. Following this success came the work of life, that of skillfully strong hands. Laura Rodig had to leave her workshop, her friends, her artistic life, to go to Magallanes, that distant and glacial place, where any art is possible with the exception of this one, and where I once saw her throw in a single night the clay crystallized by the cold, with a gesture of infinite grief.

Two years of unproductive work; but not everything was lost in vain. Her readings during that time gave to her art something that was still lacking: absolute consciousness, self-confidence. Up until that point, she had achieved exceptional marvels by intuition; now she knows what she wants; she knows her soul, she has felt her sensibility groping in the dark of hours of spiritual introspection, as one sees from the shore the immense palpitation of the sea. In only a few months of repose, three works have come out of her hands and are to be admired in this annual juried exhibition: a vigorous and, at the same time, elegant bust of F. S.; a self-study, a note of ideality that emits illusion; and an exquisite and admirable head she has called "Grace.".

Like everyone, she has reflected on the definitive border of her temperament. Today she knows that, like Donatello, she carries within herself the simultaneous desire for gentleness and strength, things only apparently contradictory; a soft and firm delicateness and a vigor without grotesque exaggerations, the tranquil vigor of the ancients.

I have seen this youthfulness burn in the flame of beauty, as others burn in the flame of the world, to live in it as if in the air and in the light, to live in it with fullness and ecstasy every day. Observing her model the humble clay with which she makes the forehead of the hero or the painful lips on a face, I have experienced the saintliness of earthen clay.

Laura Rodig possesses the sense of this divinity of Art, which will endure until men have broken impiously their last God; she feels that it is a form of religion, that it can even be by itself a purifying religion, capable of cleansing the heart, fiber by fiber.

She is modest, by the force of her talent and of her youth. She knows that no one at age twenty creates the definitive work, and she prepares herself unfeverishly for that work of art in which she will leave the eternal mold of her soul.

For me, one of the things that reveals the spirit of the soul is the capacity to admire, the continual ardor before beauty both great and small and before her diverse and at times conflicting phases. Laura Rodig is an individual made for inspiration. There is no venom in her judgments; rather, a profoundly genuine joy for the triumph of a companion. Moreover, there is the passionate cult of the masters, the names of Rodin and Mestrovic always laced with her impressions and her artistic creed. The two of them: the Latino and the Slav, the former with a ray of Greece still on his forehead and the other with his insane vision of the contemporary spirit.

I have here, then, a beautiful spirit that appears among our people. They are so rare that when one finds them it is necessary to give them the full understanding that they themselves have not gone to ask of the Philistine, and one must point them out to those who are inclined to pass by the work of young artists simply because of their tender age.

In the land of Rebeca Matte and of the chiseled cordillera, there should appear one more sculptor who gives to us one day the vast splendor of other eternal marble sculptures worthy of being placed next to those by Plaza and Simón González.

(Santiago, December 18, 1920)

MARTA SALOTTI

THE EXILED

From time to time the Atlantic wave or a gust from La Plata brings some friends of mine from as far away as Guanabara [a Brazilian port]. They come to savor Brazil and enjoy her eternal Palm Sunday, which rather than bringing closure to Holy Week is prolonged for a month, a year, or eternity, for that matter. Given the distances in space and time, they also come to perform works of compassion: "To console the disheartened," from which originates this other effort: "To sympathize with those exiled from their land and language." Languages are veritable countries, even though they lack geographical features. Languages are invisible territories like religion, and like religion they are powerful. Just as physical countries have inhabitants and nomadic peoples, so do the invisible territories of languages. Each day, the inhabitants eat and nourish themselves with their verbal rice and lentils while the nomads either starve for substance and wither away to phantasms or are rescued through the generous assistance that arrives from time to time, in the form of either friends or books.

Among the Robinsonian guests that come to my house, I prefer, as with everything, those of my two professions. They afford me company through our shared experience, and their words restore motion to my numbed tongue, which has been silently impaled during twenty years of living abroad, melting within me the iceberg of my crippled Spanish and releasing it into a joyful waterfall. What a marvelous thaw!

Several years ago, upon introducing me to Marta Salotti at a gathering of Argentine scholars, Pedro Henríquez Ureña told me: "She is your family, an Argentinean relative that you have never met." This man, who was wise in

125

many aspects of life, was certainly not mistaken this time. The teacher nodded in acknowledgement and began speaking with us. Marta Salotti immediately became my Argentine source for news, books, and health issues. It was as if Ureña had seen in my face the malnutrition of the errant wanderer, the dark night of verbal displacement of the inhabitant of the land, and motioned for someone who would and could assist me; there are those who want to but cannot help, and others who are able yet unwilling.

SARMENTISM

Thanks to her efforts, the Argentine boat now almost always brings me a new book about which I have not heard anything or an old book I lost sometime during my travels. It is because of her that I have renewed my interest in Ricardo Rojas, whose essential writings many times have sustained me; because of her, another Argentine book arrived with forceful, elegant prose that has revived the restless spirits of three continents; because of her, I have known the exact hour of the arrival of the civil and religious poet, Luis Bernárdez; because of her, I also have recuperated the beloved Banchs, who in his negligence had not been re-edited; and, finally, because of her correspondence, my native language has returned to me like a flock of storks with the same animation and passion.

But when Marta Salotti does not write for a long time but instead arrives in person, the joy could not be more complete, and upon my home falls an impenetrable avalanche from the Andes. Then the elderly titan enters through these doors in the guise of this daughter of his, who installs herself extensively, and for three months of vacation this crafter of native lands and tongues skillfully commands the conversation and discourses articulately upon literary texts.

UNITY, ABOVE ALL ELSE

The antiunionists, those Hispanic Americans who show their disgust towards individuals that believe in the solidarity that was destroyed in 1810, must feel overwhelmingly disheartened at the sight of two elderly teachers addressing their children as equals even though they belong to entirely different worlds, as if divided by iron and copper walls. It would incite them to hear these teachers speak about their work and everyday matters with such earnest intimacy, correlating ideas as in the conjuncture of the hand and the forearm. That which is different, even though it is adequate—prairie opposed to valley, wheat in contrast to copper, the Atlantic surf set against the Pacific tide—these opposing visions and tendencies are dispelled like dreams, where mountains melt, split apart and allow us to pass through.

Marta Salotti's life is divided into two halves like a piece of fruit: one half is her joyous freedom and the other, her celebrated scholarly service. At eighteen years of age she rode the crest, in other words, she graduated from Normal School. At forty (unbelievable the delay!), she was named second in charge of primary education in Bueños Aires.

Perhaps the most striking feature of this urban woman is her tanned skin, toasted to the point of appearing like a raisin from the Mendocina region, which evokes images of vacations at the beach or in the mountains. (So busy is she that she does not bother to restore the damage incurred by the sun and surf...)

To her children she gives youthfulness in its entirety, without the distractions of young women or the stinginess of older ladies, instilling in them a handful of conflicting yet complementary virtues, as her father Sarmiento once did: impassioned furies and sensibility, experience and childish innocence, absolute certainty and flexibility. She was pioneering in her advancements in the uncharted terrain of methods and somewhat of a missionary in her total elimination of possessions; she is endowed with a lighthearted spirit which enables her to arrive unharmed in the Far West, and so imbued with an understanding of eternity that she is neither daunted nor debased by the worldly.

She walks with a spritely, confident stride that I have seen in three women of the Pampa, which tends to leave its mark on individuals: in Victoria Ocampo, her master and female model; in a child of White Bay, and in Marta Salotti. The three women strut with the swiftness of ostriches drinking from the Pampa, giving testimony in their stride to the space and freedom that are their genuine father and mother.

This Argentinean school teacher speaks at first in the smooth tongue characteristic of professors, yet it isn't long before she suddenly switches to another discursive mode, a verbal canvas created by the Pampa, her beloved wet nurse. This alternative mode of conversation of Marta Salotti, incredible woman of Bueños Aires, brings out nothing less than her concern for her nation's agricultural system: she speaks of black specks on the Franciscan humus, the composer of wheat; the seven grains that someone, I forget who, once enumerated; the fragrance of trampled grass; some magnificently silken horse hair that is the legacy of the gauchos; infinite seashells washed up on the shore, and the large nocturnal dewdrops that hang like a divine breath above the earth, which, by virtue of its adopted christianity, is all the more humanitarian.

I regret that this all may seem like nothing more than idle comparison, yet it could not be more true: my colleague speaks precisely in this way, as if grooming the farm's invisible lamb, and the individual who hears her is the recipient of all that has been animated, invigorated, and recently sheared. It seems that each day Marta Salotti has just arrived from the Pampa without having passed through Bueños Aires to disembark nor through customs, where she would have had to surrender some of her rural cargo. I have never known a schoolteacher whose discourse is so profoundly rooted in the earth; nor have I seen, in all my countless ventures through the rural countryside, a farmer that conversed in this fashion, with such a vast knowledge of a region's flora and fauna. It is because of this awe that I sing her praises, as if she were a marvel of the Argentine soil, sea, and air which arrives to me in Brazil in an onslaught of waves, a gust of wind, and finely ground herbs.

When the futurist painters present models sketched from their professions or passions, they don't go about it in jest but rather record precisely what they see. One would have to paint Marta Salotti composed of numerous segments extracted from the earth, or overflowing amidst the flowers: a brushstroke of vines here, another larger figure of wheat fields with the fluttering of wings propelling her bare arms.

SUBTLE SEARCH

On her last trip she brought me a book that I devoured in small bites, lingering over every passage, in much the same fashion that the dove spaces apart her seeds so as to lengthen the enjoyment. The book (*The Teaching of Language*, written in collaboration with Dr. Carolina Tobar García, whom I've never met and thus will hold comment) deals with matters that always invoke for me the worst of memories: those of the scholastic composition. (My eyes have consumed thousands of notebooks, but to no one's advantage, as it is utterly useless to correct writing if the inorganic mode of thinking has not been addressed within the classroom and children have not been broken of the habit of lying, that is to say, twisting the facts, to accommodate their version of reality.) Regardless, I continued to read and read, knowing that little by little, that my agreement with my colleague and companion stemmed from many years of experience, and similarly from many common fears. In 230 pages, Argentina is animated, like the farmer's wife bothered by the swarm of wasps, against the complete contamination of the juvenile language created by pedantic pedagogues injured in the bloody battle waged between the urban discourse and the familiar language of the rural and the domestic.

Marta has relentlessly persisted in her headstrong efforts to realize the good that God and his people have given to her. She pursues it during recreational periods, in the classroom, in the neighborhood, in the city and in the tremendous heap of notebooks and foreign texts, where others have merely reduced the conflict to nothing short of disaster. Something has been resolved for her already, but she is only beginning to undertake a vast investigation of the language in terms of its usefulness in society. In Argentina, the head of this enormous investigation is Amado Alonso, who has steadily increased the number of individuals in his collegial group of investigators at the Institute of Philology.

Marta Salotti, strong-willed yet serious intellectual, has taken as her destiny the bad seeds that exist within the educational establishment. The students' compositions have revealed to her in confidence certain facts that the keepers of language neither see nor hear and which everywhere are escalating from bad to worse. Her book is not overly indulgent, nor is it too heavily weighted with theory. Even though she does incorporate theories of her own and others, all of superior caliber, with an honesty that honors the profession, her preference is to undertake the works themselves. Her book is almost like an x-ray: examining the verbal organism of children in its healthiest condition, exploring the damage incurred by academic grafts' slow but lethal linguistic shifts, and finally in the analysis of language overtaken by uneducated slang. The child continues to abandon domestic speech—as Guillermo de Torre has termed it—for fear of embarrassment, adopting the discourse of the classroom, which denies one the invigorating juices that have nurtured the child for over seven years. This pretentious, unnatural linguistic dress is not becoming on the child, just as the notary's clothing hardly suits the gardener; yet the child, anxious to please and adulate, seeks to obey and earn favor, and does so, but at cost of losing that which is most dear upon arrival at school: the will and desire to create, and the natural elegance of expression.

Not only does the poor child pay this tremendous price for one's own authentic mode of expression, but also the themes that will be of most interest to this child are not those of one's choice, rather those suggested or recommended by others, alas: always, the seasons, although one from the city rarely sees these different faces; and always "the Nation" in the form of a theological abstact; love for school, to which it is necessary to sing in litanies even though one detests it; the stroll through the countryside, a colorful countryside; and maternal love, stamped with doctrinaire catechism, never the genuine mother of flesh and blood. And other such themes that we have all had

129

to endure and that still haunt our battered memories.

The schoolteacher with a critical eye is pained by conventional compositions as rigorously structured as electoral speeches that either contain the
most horrendous rhetoric—that of the nineteenth century—or, by avoiding it
completely, are transformed into the hardened brick of schematic pedagogy.

The harsh criticisms of the book have offered, consequently, many negative
conclusions. I will extract this one, for instance, among the many admonitions: the student lacking the courage to be creative thus merely repeats the
ideas of others, in the same manner that a pedestrian walks instead of run-
ning out of human respect. Marta Salotti prods and encourages the child,
stimulating and inspiring him, finally hurling him headlong into unbound creativity with her magical exercises. There is something in these exercises that
resounds, a powerful and effective launching of the imagination akin to the
casting of the stone or the shot of an arrow. The child's imagination once
released, skips and then flies, and doesn't fall until it has completed its para-
ble. This gymnastics or mischievous play is for those who do not falter easily,
and weeks later, the trainee will have lost all fear and let go of creature comforts and will fling himself into the game without pushing or screaming, as
does the swimmer who has overcome his fear of water.

The passion that Marta Salotti has put into her impulsive pedagogical mission intrigues and inspires me. She seems to be at once a philologist, a writer
and a soul bearer; that is to say, she apparently shares the same missionary
zeal of those who explore the delicate nature of our language, carrying within
them the ability to see the most intimate regions of the soul. It is not surprising that Professor M. Marouzeau of the Sorbonne, has said that her book,
Instruction of Language, would give infinite pleasure to M. Bally and to other
European scholars.

A MORE ETHICAL AESTHETICS

Marta Salotti, a teacher by trade, is also a profoundly religious soul. She
gives careful consideration to the notion that forced acceptance by children of
the language that they are taught in schools will guide them toward deceit-
fulness. From her experience, seasoned over many years, as with the palm
tree, she acknowledges that the childish lie cripples man and debilitates the
human race. The European tends to speak of our Creole lifestyle as a pretty
gathering of mischief, cunning, and hypocrisies that weaken civil life, com-
mercial endeavors, and all courtly forms of life. This teacher wants for her
school a classroom and a patio filled with children resonating with verbal

freedom and dynamically extravagant actions.

There is still more to her endeavors as a gardener in her attempts to conserve the straight stalk of the infantile word. She has discovered—perhaps in herself—the happiness that results from remaining loyal to her Spanish-American linguistic heritage: a happiness acquired through the particular joys afforded by this language; through the sweet savoring that only she can offer to us for our vast repertory of visual and auditory experiences; through the delights of her intimacy: all in all, through the act of conveying those materials which this very dynamic individual passionately undertakes.

THE GIFT OF SPEAKING

Thus speaks this professor from Buenos Aires, in a language marbled with urban maturity and rural infancy, and her not having abandoned her original, authentic mode of expression must be the secret to her fascination over children.

To hear her tell a story about an expansive ranch or describe a small prairie animal, which she can bring to life with her words, or to hear her relate her chats with the children, is equivalent to mysteriously arriving at the farm and following the trail of a small rodent through rough terrain and bad weather.

Her genius resides in her speaking ability, which to me is more valuable than writing, because it is equivalent to taking an angelic mold of everything without losing any of the pieces, and it is an uncommon virtue in our people of oral tradition, a tradition that is bleeding a slow, agonizing death. In my colleague, this ability has not been lost, but rather, is just as much a part of her as her ability to breathe or walk. She was never taught this ability but has always possessed it.

If the normal schools would attribute to the oral genius the sublime qualities that it exercises in the academic spirit; if they were to understand how much influence they have on children, winning them over through the vibrant fibers of graceful speech, the children's resistance in the academic battle would be quelled, and the climate of the classroom, now of boredom and tension, would be completely changed as if by sorcery.

Marta Salotti aims to achieve one more goal with her preaching of the natural language in the child. She knows as well as Unamuno that rhetoric is virtually a thing of the past, that in the coming era, of engineers and mechanics, the aristocrat, first Roman, than that of the eighteenth century, then the Jacobean no longer possesses the probability of getting ahead. The nobility lost its solemnity and candor in the hands of the romantics, and no one believes in their parliamentary persuasions or teachings. On the other hand, the conversational Spanish of the former Basque has served to brighten human intellectual capacity on any given morning in September.

This verbal virgin, dauntless like the "the cowgirl of the Finojosa," is the scholarly muse of Marta Salotti. The compositions in her book give testimony to the conquests of a teacher of the highest caliber. The animated sentences of this modest editor are rapid, passionate and graceful; reverberating like the wings of a hummingbird, not giving into the idling of run-on sentences nor dawdling in pointless comings and goings, embracing, nonetheless, pranks and mischievous play. But sobriety does not excite or stimulate; this childish prose is, like the quintessential child, pure action. Marta Salotti emphasizes the "affective language," but in truth, she diminishes the sentimentality of the text with corrections: her children write in the objective and decisive manner used by artisans, ceramists, weavers, and carpenters. They write with precision in addition to using idiomatic expressions and clever interjections. These children say that the concrete world is theirs, without inventing "states of being" like the miserable poets, and they express their ideas with directness, with the swiftness of a brook that flows vertically.

The texts written by young women smell of domestic spaces, such as the home, the kitchen, and the dining room: they confer a real sense of the things among which they live. As such their writing resembles—forgive me the expression—the blouse recently removed, the armchair upon which one leans, or the rind of an entirely peeled orange, by the warmth of life that fills the reader. Their subject matter is joyful and animated, and they do not hesitate to express themselves, because nothing, whether it is work or play, restrains a child. (That is for those of us who are older.)

I think of the Peguys, the Ramuzes, the Gionos, which Marta Salotti is fostering in her schools, without instructing solely on the basis of "rules."

TWO PATRON SAINTS

When reading compositions, I often remark to myself that it is a blessing to be among a people of very articulate grandparents. Genuine Argentines never curse—nor forget, which is another form of blasphemy—two of their ancestors: José Hernandez and Sarmiento. They carry them ostensibly or covertly, continuing to nurture themselves from them since they had not exhausted the pastry or the vineyard of either one. They still persist in giving of themselves; not only do they impart vocabulary and direction, but also the method of managing reality. Their craft, if not diminished or forgotten, becomes a recipe of sorts, and helps us in whichever undertaking: novel, "corrido," chronicle, and even newspaper reporting.

THE JOY

Argentines are not, by nature, disagreeable; yet they are not jovial like the Italians or the Andalusians. Nevertheless, the person from Buenos Aires of whom I am about to speak was born under a sign of mirth, almost of euphoria. I highly regard her pedagogical culture, and I genuinely admire her exemplary academic position; but her gift of joy is one that I consider an indescribable virtue. To have supported the school on her shoulders for twenty years without panting, as one who bears the air and the sky; having withstood a marriage, equally as long, to the academic sphere while conserving entirely the youthfulness of the heart; to pass unscathed through the desolate country of pedagogy without collapsing from fatigue or boredom, all of it amazes me, just as the obstinate hope of men marveled the Eternal Father of Péguy. The block of malachite of this marvelous joy and faith of framed songs, guarded among the faithful and unfaithful, the scholars and bumpkins, unnerves me in my attempt to comprehend. Not even a powerful salvation suffices as an explanation. The climber of steep, rocky hills and the woman that wearies herself everyday among books and children, healthy and sick, has now weakened the fortress that was given to her by her grandparents and her hearty grassland. I fluctuate in my effort to understand, I remove pieces, as if in a game of chess, and Palma Guillén, who knows far more than I, says to me, "She does not have the founded joy, which is fragile; it does not come from the muscles or the sun, as in the case of the athlete; she would have borrowed it in such a case. Hers is a Christian grace, of immaculate evangelical ingredients. She wants and obtains her joy; like the true Franciscans, with time she knew that foremost was the 'acceptance with rejoicing.' Her idyllic joy with the difficulties of her profession comes from always observing this world in terms of the light of another."

The explanation that has me turning around twice in circles like the good daughter of Thomas, the man of flesh and blood, turns out to be straight as an arrow. It is certain, I tell myself: there it is. But immediately, another questions dawns on me: How is the achievement going to be repeated in a society of millions if the recipe is confused with grace, and the latter never covers the entire legion but rather settles on the heads of a few?

The spectacle of a rich and determined spirit, one, which, according to the layman, arranges itself around a specialty and, according to religion, around a mission, always attracts me and holds my attention. There is no earthly land-scape that affords such an abundant loan of moral voltage in order to jolt us and launch us off onto our mission of redeeming actions.

THE TREE OF MUSIC

Any enterprise that examines the word, the mystic might call Verb and attempt to extract from it all trivialness, crudeness, or deception, revealing love and beauty toward the soul. These medical hygienists of expression work in all divisions of the adult language; but I have yet to encounter a vigilante working exclusively with the language of children. A child is named, animated and filled with air, and the truth is that, in the case of the majority, he trails behind us since we do not allow him the take the lead.

Marta Salotti, schoolteacher unencumbered of union noise and liberated of literary vanities, is—and has been for the past ten years—put to the arduous task of divine botany: to care for our "tree of music," which is language evolved from its first nursery. She knew from experience that the "rumored plant" was eaten by worms and spoiled since the first days of kindergarten, which was her first academic journey. Surely the spiritual and physical tenderness she felt for the children comes to her from having adopted them in the garden of infancy, which is almost like receiving them at birth. Within her zeal there is a mater-nal instinct, along with an aesthetic godmother, and an additional dose of wet-nursing, as she is aware of what negligent relatives have failed to see. The mul-tifaceted vigilance of their flesh, feelings and intellectual development, which extends from the styling of the hair and clothing to the sifting of the word, astounds me, and I have wanted to break it into pieces for my own enjoyment as well as for others.

Marta Salotti will grow old working on Argentine intimacy, obliging her people in much the same fashion, but also those who had made a profession of verbal expression. In the grand loom in which earth and sky are woven, in the good cause of the Spanish word, she touches a swarm of hands without seeing or knowing, blind like the bees of the empty hive. Better than working in blindness and ignorance would be to share ideas and exchange opinions. I have never seen, in a world full of congresses, an appointment made for the teachers and writers to discuss the business of common language. It is a civil war of competitors: the teacher that believes him or herself to be the natural master of the children, and the writer who believes him or herself to be the overseer of the adults. Pity that the latter receives his readers already disfig-ured by scholarly texts, and that the first does not know that she does not educate, but uneducates, does not nurture, but rather weakens the genius and verbal credit with the academic diet, the wit and verbal skill of Peter Pans and Alices.

In a typical school in Buenos Aires, alone and happy as if she were accompanied by legions, Marta Salotti, daughter of an armchair Sarmiento, which suffices to sustain the education of others as well as herself, continues gathering and annotating her precious experience with the children. She just finished the second book on her curious expertise; she will continue at the task until the subject matter, as profound and obscure as the deepest sea, reveals to her its beauties, its surprises, and its absurdities. She will persevere in the task until her eyes grow tired, discovering baffling anemones, unsuspected verbal starfish, acidic sturgeons and octopuses that we never have imagined, and all in an oceanic background, submerged in the blue waters that we call "infancy." They have nothing that is simple and easy for the ordinary arm to capture; the waters of infancy are hard to cut off, even more difficult to channel, and practically impossible to reduce to a list of definitions.

THE ARGENTINE ELEMENTARY SCHOOL

Since the days of Sarmiento, the founder, this school represents a kind of fourth power, a scattered capacity, without personal appeal, that spreads from the primary institution of Jujuy to the academy in the Land of Fire. Elementary education is similar to the wit and wisdom of the Argentine, the affirmation and seasoning of the nation, which has enabled it to evade corruption and destruction. It is broad and white, dispersed from the twentieth meridian to the fifty-fifth, and in showing her to strangers, it is necessary to take some crystals from the palm of her hand. The intention of this humble *recado* is to evoke in Marta Salotti's name the liberating, creative, and purist impetus of the Argentine elementary school.

Of the deceitful changes that immigration brought to Argentina with its daily infiltration, the most visible was the breakdown in the language. Writers and professors sounded the alarm, revealing their disgust with their irritated documented accent; Capdevila, with his scholarly, irritated accent. The national teaching association gathered the message and recommendations and put an end to the immense production of impalpable cereal that is popular speech. In no more than fifteen years, a palpable capsizing has been verified, which we foreigners follow closely in books and in the press. Prose and poetry have entered into some harsh rigors of conscience, doubts, and even refinements.

The teaching profession worked there hard and well: the job is not finished yet and that is to be expected: the enormous gnawing and pummeling organism of immigration continues to grow, receiving European masses, and after the war the deposit will undoubtedly double. It is not something to be announced with sirens and horns. There exists a formidable effort to warn and save at this point our childlike continent, and it is called the national school, the tight netting at once federal and unitarian, of thousands of Argentine academic institutions.

(Petrópolis, March 1944)

ISADORA DUNCAN

"Isadora died when her art was declining and she no longer succeeded in raising the ancient waves of fervor that she once knew," declared the French press, moments ahead of her slightly cool death. In truth, Isadora died in a timely fashion, when Paris moved on to the insipidly inferior dance of Josephine Baker, when, by force of the condescension for Yankee inclinations—which are, in themselves, atrocities—Paris just turned over, like a go-between, to her best salons a dance antithetical to her own.

Isadora was also a Yankee, but an Irish one, and at any rate, she was from a generation that did not agree with the dealings of slave traders. The blacks took a different revenge on the English of North America: those who traveled in special carts like oxen; those who ate separately, prayed and existed, and weren't allowed to hug the body of a white woman without the sons of Lynch descending upon them and leaving them upon the pavement the only white-ness they possess, that of their brains. They have communicated to their enemy, the reader of the Bible, the superwhite as some have called him, their rattling of impure entrails and have created for them beastly rhythms, with which New York now awakens, seizes the day and sleeps.

Isadora left the enormous dancehall of the charleston, which has the whole world crazed, at an opportune time and with God knows what elegance of fleeting finesse. Upon seeing the owners of the salons totally inebriated, she opened the door and slipped away.

Why isn't there an angel sent to watch over a select few and to choose the best time for them to depart from this earth? It would be a genuine angel of compassionate death because it would be solicitous, not like the other angel of death with whom we live, but one who would come when it was time for us to die and relieve us of our pain. It must have been that very angel who took Isadora. So happy was the angel about its achievements that it chose the day and hour well, precise like a Pythagorean entity, and as zealous as a vehement friend of the heavens. The stage is now entirely free to play black mirror games of Baker's cabaret. The deceased never succeeded in reaching one tenth of her clientele, it's true. That body of hers had turned monochromatic, like a column that, when discovered, gives the impression of an ivory yawn to the eyes of the beholder. Her veiled games—of the most noble veils ever crafted by your French artisans—bored them like the art without physiological purpose which was sought after throughout the Parisian nights. Her body, an insinuation of a pure tree, of a healthy, organic line, a body with the desire to suggest the sublime hills of Italy, France, and of every landscape, was already becoming a bit "pompier" for those who expeditiously had abandoned that orange expressed from nature...

It reminds one of the "pendant" of the two Yankees. In addition to her Irish blood, Isadora descended from another race that is an adopted culture. She came from the passionate Greeks. This other comes from the cellar of species to which the bestial forces stoop—dynamic resonances themselves—that we suffocate each day and toss aside like a loathsome mosquito, and which are stored by some secret of physics unknown to me, emerging one day with both body and name, transformed into a body and name.

Josephine Baker also belongs to the documents of our time. Her case of personal success is useful as proof that we have emptied our minds like pockets of all our aesthetic theories. That the hips and belly of Josephine Baker give pleasure to the "elite" whites implies that whatever they do not appreciate we despise or view with indifference. I always ask myself what comes after the "Josephine Baker document." "The darling of most divine backside is coming," says one cynic, "arriving from Sudan to collect ten little blue francs in Paris." Perhaps she'll come, perhaps not, but with a long stride of patience, another Isadora much more slender, fluid, and elastic, another who pertains to the realm of water in which, much to our relief, zoology is forgotten. Because tedium, that demon which made Baudelaire love the woman from Java frenetically, both instills fear and immerses us in our pleasures, one cannot chew the strong tobacco of the black dance for long without opening a window. Recently I overheard a young man confess his disgust: "It's enough to make one want to read mechanical and even geological books, if you will, instead of all that filth in jaundiced garb with its little gang of pornographic propensity." Perhaps indeed we are headed toward a better world of celestial sensuality and beauty with our beloved Pythagoras, passing through the night clubs that smell like the powdered faces of men and women, of Josephine Baker, the physiological muse.

In that way may the deceased be consoled, the supreme white dancer, as she has been designated by those who make of the other a hemisphere of dance. May her name cleanse her people. She came from the Yankees still close to Whitman and Emerson, and when she appeared in Europe, everyone marveled at her graceful neck, without any signs of wrinkles or fatigue. She was, we would be better off saying, between Whitman and Emerson, at the point in which paganism attempts to transcend to something else. Both tendencies would often separate within her, according to the interpreted moves. She could say like the great Delmira, "At times I am all soul and other times I'm all body." But her wish was almost always, according to the design of the weaver, to cross, in triangular fashion, the body with the idea of each happy movement. Even in the reveling she endeavored to return to symbolism, and this desire freed her entirely to fall into the movements of an animal. For some critics this passion to transcend disserved her. Not entirely; she guarded it from dark felinism, from the grimacing of the male ape, from the preponderance of exposed belly and backside over shoulders, neck and feet. Naturally all of this—the emphasis on a hand as expressive as the lines of the mouth, which is the very flower of the spirit, over the flashing navel used so freely by Josephine Baker—was merely a genuine predilection for a superior art form that always opts for the most authentic of means, even though these are not the most direct nor the most effective in terms of their influence on the repulsive masses.

When she appeared on the Parisian scene, the tedious choreography of the Italian schools owned the stage. At first her style was perceived as slightly pedantic. For the more modest, she also appeared too sensual due to her audacity—which in truth is simply loyalty—to reveal a nude body that ballerinas still covered with a tutu measuring at least ten centimeters. Worlds spin rapidly, especially that of dance, and the total style of Isadora, twenty years later, has come to represent the essence of decorum.

She has left behind her a universe of gestures and attitudes in which she is, now that we remember her, like an almond, firm and ivory. Steady is the agile, lithe Isadora! We continue to group her expressive gestures and rhythms around the immutably celestial body of Sirius. They continue to live in the air for us, like the rhythms of grand poets who, following their lead, continue to move individuals, unyielding, carrying with them supernatural impulses throughout this century, if not longer.

If we think about her in her lengthy niche, slender and milky cell, for her—the most svelte—it's like a sower of expressive gestures upon the land that she now succeeds in restricting. Daisies could blossom in the most unsuspected forms, violets of unedited circuits, all under her touch.

It is more difficult with her than with any other deceased individual to enter into the meaning of definitive inertia, of the obedience to existing forms and lines. Maybe the strange death that fate dealt her was violent because the other type of death, the gradual submersion of the white water-lily in the pond, the death that slowly and agonizingly drains the body of energy, was impossible for her, the erect and ephemeral one, as she has succeeded in evading it like the serpent filled with wisdom.

(February 1928)

SELMA LAGERLÖFF

Today she celebrates the passing of years—nothing short of seventy—there in her Stockholm lined with gray canals, our Selma Lagerlöff, the honor of us all.

Not the first to be honored, if we begin to consider the Nordic country; nor the first because she was weighted in her seventy years with literary experience. First in terms of literature produced by women and with only the twin figure by her side, who resists the dignity of the magnitude: with the pseudo-Nordic Madame Curie, Polish woman at home among the French people.

To commemorate her, stamps have been issued today which I place in a row so that they dramatize for me her aging. Her face appears somewhat fatigued, and the sweet haughtiness of the thirty-something eye that I once knew has softened somewhat. But the white mass of bouffant hairdo—only on her does it not appear unattractive—gives her an air of reverence, a head much more legitimate than the other, as if she were a female literary pontiff.

To lend credibility to the famous feminine solidarity, today in this city and in many other civilized towns, we ought to get together to talk about her, about the one who with grace and beauty has fulfilled a handsome number of years; to speak fondly of the all the good that she has done for us, which is so much: to review briefly for her the events of her life, which consists of a small show-case of anecdotes, and also to compose for her a somber and moving telegram: "The women of Chile—or Colombia or Ecuador—remember you, Selma Lagerlöff, and today we are reading five of your fables and dearly hope that they will revive you and give you new life."

But the truth is that we women only get together and bump elbows with elected officials to obtain the right to vote, or to organize works of charity that are treated like rocks, and the charity of Selma is not attained in that manner.

141

Since we are on the road to restoring to the word its original meaning (right, Péguy?), we may talk about "the charity of Selma Lagerlöff."

When they live touching the polar circle with their heads, certain peoples are called "too childlike," "presumptuously youthful," "vigorously prosperous." The Latin American nations, these crafty, resourceful sorts, have been Selma's kind in their excavating, penetrating and establishing traditions for their people. The tradition that the charlatans of the south forget is not the Greek nor Roman tradition, but the tradition of honoring coins that sound like legitimate metal four thousand years later.

Charity is what I call the giving of profound gifts to the needy; more than that, it is giving of a supernatural sort. Allow me, then, to insert into the category of charity the work of Selma Lagerlöff and to continue to give my reasons so as to make myself understood.

It often seems to me that peoples of the world have either high esteem or contempt for the imagination. This esteem is acquired from mythology—with the addition of folklore—and is almost more desirable than the simple, unpolished, unadorned honor of knowledge.

Peoples of myths, who give substantial weight to fables and legends, are peoples with power over those of limited imagination. Before the birth of mythology in Greece, there was that of India and China and perhaps Persia; after Greece, the Slavs and the Germanic peoples, and then after them our very own American folklore, so very distant from the Roman myths, characterized by utilitarianism, shrewdness and sophistry.

When I observe Selma on the stamp—which is how I go about knowing people—she strikes me as a graceful, prudent individual, with a resemblance to that of a snake charmer. Scandinavian legends are buried deep within her caves and her brambly thickets. (Caves are the equivalent of concentrations; thickets equate with confusion). She merely sits down to invoke them, and the firm, agile serpents begin uncoiling their bodies, slither suspiciously out into the open, approach her cautiously and finally end up on her lap to allow her to fondle them, to become acquainted with them, and to bolster her faith in them. He who is repulsed by the dear image of entwined serpents on the stamp in remembrance of she who was so impish may change them and replace them with other timorous, colorful beasts, just as long as they are somewhat magical in any event, because myths always must be somewhat submerged in mystical waters, and Selma, Swede and all, must possess something of the spirit of nature, such as a wood nymph or the mother of the elves, to be able to work with colloquial language, which is the repository of things both mystical and demonical.

An absolute humility, which could only come from a woman, made her abandon the ideas offered by her own imagination and the topics most dear to her—which surely must have returned to haunt her many times—wanting for them to be honored by her prose. She has retained that sort of second lap, which is the female mind. She has surrendered it entirely to the masses of folklore devotees who requested it with exclusive appetite, with a kind of selfish authority. There is a wealth of authenticity and transparent humbleness in the folklorist, most particularly in this female; and we should praise, along with the clarity, the duality of her art, whose creation resembles the twin halves of sliced fruit placed side by side.

Selma gives the illusion of having stopped telling tales; of having written what was dictated to her, as was customary for the ancient transcribers; of having lent her hand or mouth. But let's not go to such lengths and be so easily deceived. Let's guard against such judgments by reading the work of Sir James Frazer, the greatest folklorist, for example, which is the essence of superstitions, fable and myth. Selma has gathered like acorns of the folkloric oak many kernels, seeds, and almonds for her stories. She has kneaded the flesh of the fruit round about that core, and has infused the skin of the fruit with color and aroma. The result is what one may term, if you like, a pseudo-creation, but one must remember that placed upon the balance on the one side is the imagination of an entire people or two, dating back some three thousand years, and on the other, the work of a lone creative individual. Wagner attained far less by arranging his myths, which he somewhat ruined with his Germanic emphasis.

Madame Selma, grand dame of letters, you have possessed and utilized generously your natural ability for storytelling, for which they called you "country girl." Simplicity reveals a greatness in any profession, and another who also holds it is the pastor that Maragall wanted, for just as the true dame walks well, so she sits well, eats well and narrates well, without the interference of any pedantry in her words or gestures.

Today a party is being given in Stockholm, just as it is in Copenhagen and in Berlin, to honor this Nordic woman, who now appears on the gold coins of the common people. Let us extend the epiphany throughout all the land wherever there are women and children and all those with a hunger for the childlike in art. The storyteller has told her tales for these three groups. At times in this wrinkled and stitched patchwork which is Europe, one sees some refreshing stretches that suffice to alleviate the jaundiced eye, spaces that

143

Selma herself has put in place. Selma is, all by herself, one of those very pieces.

When titles are allocated—titles of maturity attained in art, of supreme wisdom of the word, or masteries that tend to result in delicate subtleties or in flurries of poetic impulse—what a lovely title they have bestowed upon you without realizing it, Selma Lagerlöff, that of the "naïve genius," of the storyteller abandoned in childhood! Isn't it true that when you overhear those "little children," you know very well that you have kept the best for yourself?

(1929)

ON CHILEAN WOMEN

At times while traveling through the mountains one discovers a house that is hidden in the interior, as if abandoned by God and by man. The intruder that arrives there knocks at the door with a pounding of fists and clamor; the door opens, and a woman beckons the newcomer to enter.

The house does not belong to any neighborhood; the nearest town is at least fifty kilometers away and everything there is in absolute Buddhist silence, interrupted by falling rocks, and in winter, by torrential rains.

But upon entering, the dreadful place is suddenly clouded as if in a dream. Because inside a fire is burning, and there is the inviting smell of food—obtained from who knows where—and a good night's sleep: there is human life and very often extremely, compassionate human life.

After only moments of looking and listening, it becomes apparent that this refuge nestled amid the heights of the vultures is the accomplishment of just one woman. The only things the Andean male does or knows how to do are to descend into the mine, to pant in pursuit of veins of ore, and to dynamite boulders. He doesn't look after himself, he doesn't succeed in building himself a comfortable nest, like that of the vulture. If he doesn't have this woman at his side, he slips day to day toward the barbarism of the first Indians. And the inclination to pure action, to action in the face of every danger, which is characteristic of the Chilean male from Lautaro to Portales, seems to captivate his female partner, wresting her from the hooks of idleness and converting her to his fellow-companion.

The woman that lives alongside her prize bird above the harshness of those summits ends up being a phenomenon, and a Chilean woman who finds herself anywhere, whether it be in the southernmost islands, or New York, or

Paris, this fair-skinned Ximena or this darker Guacolda join forces and cover half the territory.

She is constantly called "temperamental," and the origin of her passion is almost always an absolute love whose flame ignites the most prudent actions and the most unbridled fantasies. This fair or dark complexioned woman follows her man to the desert of salt, without complaining to him for her exile; this valorous woman raises six children in the Central Valley, stretching a salary that is only sufficient for two; she tends to emigrate so as to not lose touch with her innate, itinerant self toward the Argentine provinces or California, where she must struggle for her daily bread among the foreigners; and if she is attractive and is able to pursue a degree, often there she also triumphs in artistic creations or in the subtle art of creating an intimate relationship.

As with the Romans, "a passion drives her" and nothing less than a passion: not a whim nor detached interests nor vices. Seeing her live in any part of the world, I am always reminded of the Greeks, who attribute to delirium a sacred, religious meaning. Among those women crazed with their bodies and those simply relaxed in a bohemian state or one of misery there goes the Antarctic Eve, glowing like the southern beacons and faithful to a rational or meaningless love: it is one and the same.

After a little conversing in a small café or in a tent of immigrants, one's eyes tend to fix on her more than on any other woman. Separating her from the other spiritless ones is a vitality that burns like hawthorn set ablaze, confirmed vertically in her upright beauty; and a certain pride of misfortune causes her to straighten up like the trampled reed.

It isn't always the ordinary couple who fled that one finds there; at times there are three or more; they constitute the triangle or the hexagon or the family: there are children born in immigration, and she knows that for each one, she and her man must multiply, in the fierce algebra of the struggle for life.

In Santiago, in the margins of the feminist meetings, women have already forced open all the iron doors belonging to the professions: she is a teller in the banks, and is not known for fraud in the accounting books; she is a doctor in the hospital and a judge for minors. Her colleagues grumbled upon admitting her, and now they regret their shameful disdain; she is creative in the novel, beautifully daring in the plastic arts, and not daunted by engineering nor the most innovative architecture.

What this tremendously meritorious woman still needs is that the laborers of the farm, when she plants or cultivates, feel ashamed that she is paid only half of their salary. What is not understandable is that the legislator still does not know that this woman typically works to maintain three children, and that these individuals characteristically are an inebriated husband or vagrant and two children of theirs; and what is irritating is that one half of the Chilean population has lived until now on the limits of the redeeming support that those mothers can exercise with respect to the management and on the limits of the liberating support that they can use on behalf of rural misery.

The sense of responsibility works and agitates our "fémina" or womanhood. Her consciousness resembles a forge: she is not appeased with minor accomplishments. She desires much more, almost everything for her children; in this aspect perhaps her virtue slips a bit toward excess. (Indulgence in maternal feminism also exists in other countries, too numerous to mention).

To speak about a feminine type from any South American country is to play perilously with generalizations. On the one hand, there are the peninsular Spanish types; on the other, all the creole Americans, and furthermore still, the mestizas or mixed breeds...a sizeable assembly of women disembarked from Cádiz: Carmen came to add levity to the remote country of stone... From stubborn Castile came the Isabels and the Crazy Juanas. A greater number arrived from the Basque country than from any other of the regions, judging by their advantageous size, which towers above the common inhabitant. Galicia apparently preferred to remain on the Atlantic strip, and it is regrettable because within a geography so burdened with melancholy, the sweetness of the Celts would be a welcomed feature.

We did not remain purely Spanish: two somewhat Saxonizing presidents imported Germans in the period when germanizing merely seemed to be europeanizing. It is there within that they all multiply with particular care to maintain the racial circle. The world yet to come perhaps will counsel such deaf individuals to pursue another course and their pretensions will fall away one by one.

The Yugoslavs arrived much later, and this invaluable artery of immigrants circulates throughout the broad Patagonia. They have brought with them such force and more physical beauty than the Germans, and they are not versed in Caucasian vanity. The Jews have been the last to arrive. There they must have scattered their leaven, which wherever it falls produces geniuses and leaders, businessmen, restless minds and reflective intellects. We give to them peace and equality with the purpose of convincing them that the earthly Jerusalem and the celestial one can indeed begin for them in the precious Central Valley of Chile.

Over the Basque-Extremaduran foundation we have placed, as will be seen, so many beams of exotic wood that in little time it will not be possible to speak of a Creole Euzkadi, rather of a chess board similar to that of the Rio Plate region. Within another century, we will be a Europe hemmed by the fringe of cross-cultures. This borderland of legitimate Americanicity is useful to us because of the proximity to the Altiplano and to the Tropics: a people of white-colored skin as desired by some individuals would disturb somewhat the brotherhood of the Pacific, and our natural destiny is indicated by that mysterious water.

It is said that the product that emerges from resisting metals condenses in women, emphasizing particular features of the face that travelers have praised in passages now considered classic. There is in her a burning look that, like fire, is applied indiscriminately to objects large and small that surround her, because everything constitutes for her the material of life for all that is regarded as essential; and typically there is a voice that rises and falls from sweetness to vehemence, always returning to sweetness. There is a tradition of serving and always serving others with the quickness of a wink of the eye and within a warmth characteristic of Pauline charity. Happiness is found in absolutely all classes, but in the country woman there dominates a peculiar oriental sorrow. (Beauty depends upon health, which beautifies just as much as happiness.) Regardless, popular dialect is seasoned with the spices and pepper of the Andalusian jester, and the craftiness of the Creole.

The futuristic currents that are circulating throughout the world already are reworking the larger cities, and are applying to the Romanesque walls of ancient times the great strikes of the catapult. The commotion of the planet reverberates as well in the Chilean Eve, rocking her and moving her toward urban centers. Her legendary temperament makes her more sensitive than the barometer to the warm climate of post-war society. Notwithstanding, the stubborn metal of her character persists, and traditional life and everything there defends itself in the same fashion as our underground silver, without gesture, and with a stern silence that is simultaneously resistance.

(Santiago, Chile, June 1946)

ON MEXICAN WOMEN

Mexican woman: nurture the child in whose flesh and spirit the Latin American race will prove itself.

Your complexion, colored richly by the sun, is gorgeous; the delicateness of your figure possesses concentrated energy, and belies your frailness. You were made to bear the strongest men, the daring conquerers, those needed by your people in their tremendous hour of danger: organizers, workers and farmers.

You are seated in a simple, contented manner in the hall of your home, where quiet and silence seem to languish; but in truth, there is more strength in your peaceful lap than in an army that passes by, perhaps because you are cradling the hero of your people.

When they tell you, Mexican mother, about other women who shake off the duties of motherhood, your eyes burn with pride, because for you the whole of motherhood is the most ineffable delight and the most complete manifestation of nobility.

When they tell you, disturbingly, about mothers who do not suffer like you with sleepless watchfulness alongside the cradle, and who do not give the life of their blood through nursing, you listen contemptuously, because you are not about to renounce the many nights of anguish spent with your feverish child nor are you willing to allow your child to drink milk from another's breast. You will always breastfeed and rock to sleep your child and continue to carry the burden of these mothers who have abandoned their children and let them fall upon your chest.

Mexican mother: to find your great role models, you must not look upon the crazed women of this century, those who dance and entertain themselves in plazas and salons and hardly know the child that they carried deep within their wombs, the selfish women who betray life by avoiding their respons-abilities without avoiding pleasure. You will turn your eyes to the ancient and timeless models: the Hebrew and Roman mothers.

Give joy to your child, that joy may fortify his or her blood and muscles. Sing to your child the sweet songs of your country; play by your child's side in gardens and in the shifting water of your bath; take your child to the coun-tryside and bask in the brilliant light of your plateaus.

They have told you that your purity is a religious virtue. It is also a civic virtue: your womb sustains the race; multitudes are born of your bosom with the silent eternal flow of the springs of your land. The debasement of men always starts with the degradation of women and it is this that muddles the river as it winds through the villages; yet their sources are pure.

Mighty and lovely is the land in which you happened to be born, Mexican mother: it has the most perfect winds in the world and gathers cotton in smooth delightful balls. You are the companion of the land, and as such you must deliver the arms that will collect the fruit and the hands that will gather the cotton. You are the earth's collaborator and consequently you are bathed with grace in the light of each morning.

Mexican mother: vigorously demand for your child all that existence owes to those who are born without asking to come into this world. For your child, you have the right to ask more than anyone, and you do not allow your request to emerge from the mouths of others. Ask for your child a bright, clean school; ask for cheery parks; ask for magnificent fountains and festivals of images, in books and in cinema; demand collaboration in certain laws; make them erase the shame of the illegitimate child, and do not permit them to let this child be born and live as an outcast, in the midst of other happy children. Demand laws that deliver to you the services of childhood benefits, those that regulate your work and that of the children who toil like slaves in brutal fac-tory jobs.

To attain this you will have to be daring, without ceasing to be prudent; your word must not be hideous, rather it will acquire saintliness and will come to pass through the multitudes that hear in you the words of the divine.

You have the right, mothers, to be seated among the schoolteachers and to discuss with them the education of your children, to inform them of their errors until they have been corrected.

Sooner or later they will hear you, Mexican mother; toward you the just men will turn, of which there still remain many. Because your majesty divides and conquers all other sovereignties, the verse of Walt Whitman is recalled when one observes you in passing: "I say that there is nothing greater than the mother of men."

The world will continue to mature slowly in terms of justice. It is true that it is already accepted that your voice rises above the voices of men, requesting on behalf of your child, who is more yours than the father's because of the greater pain that you have endured for the child's sake.

I love you, Mexican mother, sister of mine, who embroiders exquisitely, weaves placemats the color of honey, and crosses the country dressed in blue like the Biblical women to carry provisions to her child or her husband, who is watering the cornfields.

I speak to you, therefore, in the same manner that I speak to the women of my race in the south, with an accent that you will not perceive as cold or intrusive. I repeat to you: the Latin American race will be tested and proven by your children; in them, all of us from the entire southern continent will be judged and saved or we will be lost. God has given them the unfortunate luck that shall enemies advance, the Northern swell shall break upon their chests. Therefore, when your children fight or sing, the southern countenances will turn toward this land, filled at once with hope and with despair.

Mexican woman: upon your knees you cradle the Latino race, and there is no greater nor more decisive destiny than yours at this hour.

(Mexico, January 1923)

MESSAGE FOR THE GUATEMALAN WOMEN'S CONFERENCE

Mrs. President and Esteemed Female Participants of the Conference,

My warmest, sisterly greetings to all you who have responded to our call and come from far away and with great sacrifice, as well as to the Guatemalan women that are homemakers and your hostesses. Immeasurable loyalty has been your response, and I have failed you, but, you must believe me, for health reasons that are totally beyond my control. I love this city, and the country of Guatemala; I have a tremendous appreciation for Central Americans, and I would have enjoyed regaling with you our North American female companions, because we owe infinite acts of kindness and favors to our neighbors from the United States.

This conference is the work of the International League of Women for Peace and Liberty. Although the motto of our society is based on certain romantic notions, if it is interpreted correctly, an impassioned reality emerges. We exist in an impoverished peace given to us by short-term lenders. We walk trembling with anxiety and as if treading tropical lands mined with invisible anthills which crumble readily under the step of rubber workers. This is, indeed, an undesirable existence, or merely a partial existence, for the most valuable treasure of the world, and that of each man, is what one would call most simply confidence, the human spirit's ability to rest in the good faith of the surrounding community.

It happens that at this very moment in the real world something most unusual is occurring, and it is a matter of us being surrounded by everyone. We were once a game with national cubes, balls and triangles scattered upon the earthly surface; and then suddenly, these pieces became ordered in a circular fashion, and now we are all either elbow to elbow or face to face, looking each other in the eye. Yet, in that semicircle which is the UN, not all of the hands are yet linked together, and if they are, the grasp is loosened by suspicion.

Our exemplary president, the exceptionally brilliant Heloisa Brainerd, looking over our times with the spyglass of a sailor, gave us peace as our first commander even during those years when we were all sleeping with the belief that the terrestrial globe was as solid as balls of iron. There was never such a metallic sphere, and she knew it; rather, it was a globe of decayed wood which could easily be ignited by the match of a madman. Then war ensued, throughout the greater part of history, the avowed total war, and it was realized in three and even in four dimensions. It was eradicated with the victory of the righteous one, and it seems as though all of the materials overturned in the catastrophe have become corrupt and agitated in just two years. Now it seems that even the soundly untouched hemisphere that is our own can also be overtaken by this infection.

Following the immaculate word "peace" in our slogan is the priceless word "freedom," and this is the weaker of the two for there was always peace on some continent, even though it might not have been peace of the good desirable kind. As for freedom, the poor world has not known this except in some more fortunate areas. Liberty has been the luxury of a few and the hunger of all the remaining others who lived watching it from afar like a little puppy eyeing a table laden with fowl.

In the name of freedom our allies made war, and the highest command was for us this ancient and virtuous word, which the world knows how to pronounce very well, like the name of God, but which never lives a true existence, as in the case of the most profoundly intimate love.

With the war concluded, it happened that, like an absent power that has been invoked, freedom raised its body and began to walk, to speak and to recover its right to possess the Earth. It is natural: freedom wishes to become once again the governess of the people God made for her and not for "mock dinners" in the palaces of Salamanzares, learned or illiterate, fair or dark-skinned.

In the year 1945 all people looked toward newly-attained freedom with excitement and euphoria, like someone who observes the sun for the first time or who suddenly notices the sea. (Even though I may have been born upon its knees in the interior of Chile, I am similarly amazed by its sheer delight).

Once freedom is experienced, it becomes the greatest passion and the most provident custom; she is truly the mother who raises the child well and yields to the human spirit; but she is also, by odd curiosity, the milk that, once drunk on a daily basis, some no longer admire nor love, nor regard as at risk and guard it with one's life. Even though she was one of our first benefactors, her attractiveness is quickly fading for many of her sons (the Europeans, for instance), owing to the insipidity caused by the sheer habit of that which they have always possessed. It is necessary to revalidate in the blurred vision of doubtful eyes this freedom which has raised us and to spell out her name to those of unfaithful ear.

But those of us who are distressed by the circumstance of this declining freedom must follow the path of its fall and investigate the causes of its loss of prestige.

You, my friends or companions in the League, are going to speak here about these two realities, enigmatic because of their intangibility, which revert the world to a miserable state when one or the other disappears: precariously unstable peace and freedom that has lost prestige in popular esteem.

I would like, due to the impotence caused by my absence, to converse with you on a subject that is always the focus of my attention. It may seem like a trivial, insignificant topic, but for the dignity of South America, it has had a profound, ever dramatic impact.

Throughout our America one hears a cry that emerges from the rocky sierras of the Indians and declares: "We want freedom with bread." Whoever hears this cry, may you descend to the depths of your conscience, a place where it is necessary to go at times, and may your pulse begin to beat wildly. It is true that dignitaries from the year 10 granted liberty, and that their successors in some southern regions defended her—at times entirely and at others, piecemeal. What they neglected to do, both the founders and the successors, was precisely that which is the essence of this cry: "bread and freedom." What a lovely alliance, and how belatedly we realize that these two words share a common meaning, and that they complement each other: freedom needs bread, for the hungry, like beasts of burden, tend to follow the first individual that shows to them a bite to eat, but bread not eaten in freedom does not nourish, and its crumbs sour once inside the mouth. Every cunning dictator who has seen this unfortunate flaw as easily as a one can detect a crack in the walls of a house, each one who has seen freedom debilitated, has kicked it aside with the tip of his boot and has begun to distribute large loaves of bread sanctimoniously, at the cost of precious flour. Commonplace individuals are not that savvy, and they didn't realize that these breads did not contain the "ineffables of freedom." In every one of our countries, for years or even decades, the rolls dispensed by the "benefactor" have caused our people to forget about their freedoms, as if these were just mindless tunes or melodies.

Peace and freedom will govern this humble battered planet if both work together, adding social justice to their classic duo. Neither peace, nor legalities, nor ethics can exist within the tight fist of hunger.

As I know far less than any one of you about the methods of social reform, I will attempt to interpret only a small component of your program, that which interests me the most. I want to remind you of the living wound that is the work of women in the tropical fields and in the Cordillera; I wish to put in the palms of your pioneer hands the diseased intestines that constitute our ultra-rural life.

With no reason other than that of being a woman and not being able to hold up high the banner of suffrage nor to approach the hallowed ballot box, the female field worker in several tropical countries earns one half to two thirds of a man's pay. It is not that, due to the alleged frailty of the female body, a woman works less than the customary ten hours; nor is it that this loyal gender knows little about sowing or irrigation, or that she picks less fruit than her husband or eldest son; in the overloading of bundles on her back, she is like the mule or donkey. This noble supporter is equal to the men in her work: she carries the firewood to the farm or transports pottery to the market with an astonishing strength. In the toilsome life of the prairie, of the savanna, of the forest or of the mountains, it is far less a question of this female individual making herself into the pampered, spoiled, or moody one, the "girl of worn hands." I have even seen women join men in clearing the railways after snowstorms or landslides of boulders from the mountains, and I have remained there observing this intently for hours, driven by this fascination that we derive from both the grotesque and the beautiful, an obsession which nails us at a certain point to punish our eyes, which only see cities and chisel the countryside out of repulsion and contempt.

In essence, it is a question of a job punished with the cut of a ridiculous deduction based on a kind of sexual taboo: woman, due to her inferiority in terms of physique, "needs to do less," according to the adage that runs from the Caribbean to the Patagonia, and should only earn one half or a third of a man's salary. The truth is that, in addition to accepting mannish tasks, she breastfeeds, prepares meals in the open field, and upon her return home, feeds the family again; and on Sundays, she sews for the children.

Three ranch owners have told me, in different countries, that women have advantages over men in agricultural labor due to the conscience that they put into their duty, and that they never miss work on Saturdays and Mondays because they are not inclined to drink.

Plain and simply, it is a question of gender, of what women are and, in this as in the professional positions, employers hold the opinion that "they spend less because they are lacking in the costly vices of men," according to the textual phrase I heard from a leftist leader when he was addressing the differences in salary between male and female teachers. Such an incredible reason strikes our ears as farcical, but in actuality, these are very serious beliefs expressed shamelessly by those who take advantage of the situation.

As for the very owners of the desolate lands that distress the eyes, they are not perverse people nor mythological monsters. I have known them since infancy and I have encountered them afterwards in some seven countries of the South. I can honestly say that they only represent the case of partial callousness by the environment and the customs into which they were born, lived and died. A hardened social injustice corresponds precisely to the degeneration of the skin, and with that, to the loss of all sensitivity (and I am not speaking about "conscientiousness" for this seems to be an unusual luxury in the common man, a spectacle as rare as the sun at midnight). Somber night is the creole camp located approximately 300 kilometers from the cities where the law keeps vigil, deters and punishes. Within the ultra-rural life of these places to which I am referring there is a kind of geology in the habit of social function, and both men and women have been seated upon those marbled boulders from the beginning of time, abusers as well as victims, men along with women. If the agitation of that land does not come from outside and under the form of social criticism, everything will remain the same, just like in the caves filled with dauntless forms that grow white with eternity.

The truncated salary of women corresponds to an Indian or Black woman of exceptional virtues and very minor flaws: she rarely drinks and she does not frequent those bars where brandy made from wood or potatoes is served. Their bloodstained money represents, in the filthy hut and pigsty, the colorless, flavorless soup that she gives to her two or five children and is the pay for a week of work that, needless to say, slips by without the slightest diversion, including card games.

Our view, however, ignores, for the sake of convenience, approximately seventy percent of the country's territory. And what we are ignoring are the mountainous areas savage from the sun and lack of rain, the marshy rice fields, or the tropical jungle, bubbling agitatedly because of all the larva and insects that swarm in the Tropics.

Walking from encampment to encampment, for these are neither towns nor even minute villages but rather an overabundance of huts quite distant from each another; dismounting and taking long rests, to observe at length out of curiosity and amazement, if one is riding horseback through this area; if you are traveling by car, you surely know that the salary whisked away from a woman, her bread sliced in half, is precisely what feeds her offspring, because the salary of a male, like water in an arid sandbank, is largely absorbed by the bar, the brothel, the cockfights and other disgraces they call "entertainment." And so, in this fashion, the ultra-camp lives in an incredible matriarchy: the family is supported by the pitchfork that is rumored to be as weak as women!

Although the aforementioned may sound like a scandalous myth, this is the true life of several thousands of Indians, mestizos and blacks living in shanties. I am not relating exaggerated or exceptional cases; I have seen, I have heard and I have experienced first-hand days of horror in rural dwellings, in an attempt to observe and comprehend before commencing to write my testimony. And everything that you are hearing causes your cheeks to burn and turn scarlet, which we call shame, because we Latin Americans are sons and daughters of Europe, or at least that is what we like to call ourselves, yet in the Old World such a life would be seen only in Arabian gypsy camps or some Asian infernos.

And what happens, one might ask, when a woman does not work because she has several children or because the plantation owner refuses to hire women? In that case, the result is that three or sometimes seven human beings exist on the drained brook that is the salary of the alcoholic father.

I ask you, with the earnest of an absentee who so wishes to be present, to graciously eradicate the offense approximating contempt directed at the work of our rural women. The reform that Feminism must demand first and foremost is that of equal pay, from the cities to the most remote hiding place in the mountains. Undertake your own private and confidential inquiries. Observe, verify or rectify "de visu," striving to immerse yourselves in the darkest of "green infernos" and the simplest of mountainous solitudes. Undoubtedly you will see purgatories, lands and people that seem to belong to another planet, and you will be confronted with a citizenship about which you never have heard a word spoken because it does not exist in the villages that are somewhat humane.

Do not believe in blinding statistics and news reports; endeavor, instead, to travel there. The geography of those places makes it possible for them to be called "the heart of country A or Z." What secret and wounded hearts! The word is only useful to designate those nestled hiding places that are similar to beavers' dens, and perhaps express the consumptive pulse of the putridly ill individual.

I hope our Guatemalan Conference will have made a defiant and effective statement within the silence, which is guarded by the patriotisms with regard to such a somber topic. Such a thick veil is draped over enormous racial sins.

The woman of the countryside and of the mountains who has passed by scarcely noticed within your view, hurried yet content, is the most helpless of our sisters. Let us initiate our first contact with her and not unbind the ties made today between her and the "International League of Women."

(Santa Barbara, California, 1948)

WOMAN'S EDUCATION

Let's reflect back on the history of humanity, searching for the silhouette of woman throughout the different periods of world history. We find her more humbled and debased as we delve in antiquity. Her eminence is marked by the same march of civilization. While the light of progress illuminates with greater intensity our world, she, woman, the oppressed one, begins to hold her head up erect more frequently.

To the extent that light is produced in moments of understanding, she, too, begins to understand her mission and her worth, and today she is no longer the slave of the past but rather one's companion, an equal. Considering her early abasement, she has advanced significantly, but there remains much to be explored and executed before intoning a chant of victory.

If in her social life she occupies a position that is befitting, it is not the same in the realm of the intellectual; her presence here, if not invisible, is excessively pale.

It has been said that a woman only needs a minimal education; moreover, there are those who still see her as merely capable of governing the home.

Her education is a major task that entails the complete reformation of an entire gender. Because the educated woman ceases to be that ridiculous fanatic who only attracts disdain; because she ceases to be that monotonous wife who, to preserve marital love, depends exclusively upon her physical beauty, which results in a loathsome life in which reflective contemplation is extinguished; because the educated woman ceases to be that helpless individual who, feeble in her fight with suffering, ends up selling herself miserably if her physical strength does not permit that work.

To educate a woman is to dignify her and exalt her, to broaden for her the scope of the future, to wrest from degradation many of her fellow victims.

It is essential that a woman ceases to be the beggar of protection and that she be able to live without having to sacrifice her happiness for a repugnant contemporary marriage, or her virtue by the disgraceful selling of her honor. Almost always the degradation of a woman is due to her abandonment and want of favor.

Why that preposterous idea of certain parents of removing from the grasp of their children's hands scientific works, out of fear that these readings will alter religious sentiments of the heart?

What more honorable religion than that of the learned and wise?

What more immense God than that One before whom the astronomer kneels, after having scrutinized the abyss from the heights?

I would make accessible to all youth the readings of all those luminous suns of the sciences, so that they might fall profoundly into the depths of the study of that nature, about whose creator an idea should be formed. I would show them the sky of the astronomer, not the heaven of the theologian; I would familiarize them with that space which is populated by worlds, not by flashes of divine light; I would show them all the secrets of those heights. And, after having known all these works and after discovering what Earth is in space, they would form their religion according to the dictates of their intelligence, reason, and soul. Why affirm that a woman only needs a basic education?

Throughout every historical period of the world in which woman has been the beast of the barbarians and the slave of the civilized, just how much intelligence has been lost in the darkness of her sex! How many geniuses might have not lived in wretched servitude, unexploited and unknown!

Educate woman; there is nothing in her that rightfully relegates her to a position of subordination in relationship to man.

Let her convey a dignity more dear to life: the dignity of enlightenment.

Let something other than virtue ennoble her and make her worthy of respect, admiration and love.

With the education of the beautiful feminine sex, all of you will find fewer miserable, fewer fanatical, and fewer helpless women.

Let science, which is the sun, with all its power illuminate her mind.

Let knowledge enable her to recognize the debasement of the betrayed and the depraved woman and endow her with strength for life's struggles.

Let her come to value herself for who she is and to cease to be the creature who agonizes and is miserable if her father, husband or son do not support her.

A greater future and more assistance for women!

Seek out all means possible so that she may live on her own without begging for protection!

As a result there will be fewer degraded women and consequently less of a shadow on that half of humanity. Moreover, there will be greater dignity in the home. Education ennobles the most base of souls and inculcates in them grand sentiments.

Persuade her to love science more than jewels or silk.

Let her devote herself to the best years of her life. Place in her hands scientific texts as one would place the Manual of Piety.

As a result she will elevate herself with majesty and dignity, she who has been helpless and degradingly humiliated.

Let glory shine in her face and her name echo throughout the intellectual world.

And alongside the educated man no longer may there be that ignorant individual who is bored by scientific discoveries and who does not comprehend the enchantment and sublimity possessed by that goddess for superior minds.

Let her be the Stela who dreams in her work, Flammarion, sharing with the astronomer the celebrated solitude of her life; the Stela who does not lament the loss of her diamonds nor lives unhappily far from the adulation that constitutes the deplorable vice of elegant women.

Honor be to those representatives of the people who include within their programs of social work the education of women; to those who endeavor to fight on behalf of the betterment of women: to them, success and victory!

(Vicuña, March 8, 1906)

THE FEMALE VOTE

The French Congress has denied women the right to vote. Lord Kirillis, one of the leaders of the conservative party's propaganda, which has the formidable ability of electoral "affiche," has launched Proposition 200, taking full advantage of the occasion: a group of working mothers with faces of defeat who continue to voice the injustices of the Left...

It is necessary to disengage the issue from the realm of interested sentiment, which, from both sides, is maimed with falsehoods. Never before has the right-wing been feminist, despite the fact that they are now, out of desperation, nor have the Leftists been sincere in their pledged adhesion to women's suffrage. In the most opportune moments both take up this banner for their own benefit.

The feminine vote is something to be discussed in the language of rights. In systems of universal or restricted suffrage, ever since the Revolution which has been termed great, the principle of popular representation was firmly established, with the understanding that the vote belonged to the human race. To discuss at length the extent of this right is not serious and, when not manifesting debasement, reveals stupidity.

Why then, has it taken us one hundred years to excite public opinion with regard to the feminist question, and why have England, Spain and Italy delayed so long in granting it?

I do not believe in the senseless rationalization of the Enlightenment that was to have brought about our vote among many of its other meaningless endeavors, just as I do not believe in the cliché of the priest snatching from us the torches of those who speak, the humble Luisa Michel: nor do I believe in men's fear of female competition in parliament, which is despicable. We women have not had the inclination for this, nor will we have them in the realm of politics.

The Catholic church, owing to a sense of regulation of the sexes and a desire to limit ordination to men, has recommended at times that women should stick to what is rightfully theirs, to their own domain, to their proper moral character. It persists—I believe—in its belief that this is most beneficial. Yet they must have seen that, without voting, without going to conferences, without sustaining electoral aspirations, women have filled their lives with strange preoccupations and that which they label sociability (to avoid calling it by its real name, gilded idleness) occupies them, satisfies them, and estranges them from their children, to the point that they would transform it into the most tempestuous political struggle, and today the Church looks without fear at the feminine vote and its advantages.

Socialists and radicals have been born into the life of electoral combat with the affirmation of equality of the sexes as a natural topic of conversation. All of their literature is versed, debated, immersed in a feminist discourse that, in essence, is suggestive of the kettledrum and of the trumpet of Jericho. While they were minorities, without the padded privileges of the government, they have maintained the feminist discourse with passionate incisiveness. But one fine day they governed, as in France, and panic overcame them at the fear of the loss of favor, always pleasing, of the press. Since then, and even though the intellectual leaders have continued to make declarations of loyalty to "the cause of oppressed woman, spurred and forgotten by political conservatism," the truth of the matter is that, possessing the ability to give an overwhelming majority for the approval of the law, they have managed to evade it, with an abundance of motives that make ingenious French feminists laugh heartily.

In countries of the North, where, it seems, leaders take a program seriously and there is often more integrity and less rhetoric from the Left, and to some extent on the part of the Right, they have carried out this agenda in due time.

The biggest surprise that Latina feminists have experienced is that of Italy and Spain. Without a dramatic display of propaganda, almost without propaganda of any kind, they have lost the prize, which the modest English women succeeded in obtaining from the British Parliament, like prey from the teeth of a leopard.

How can one comprehend that the reason for Mr. Mussolini's and General Primo de Rivera's feminist zeal is very different than that of Juaréz or that of M. Blum. It is exceptionally difficult to understand how a general, who is, moreover, a Spaniard, in other words, one who may well possess the most sophisticated code of traditionalism, could embrace with passion the feminist cause, which bears the mark of his natural enemies...

Mr. Mussolini was a socialist, and a militant socialist in journalism. It may be that this aspect of socialism remained with him, although it is difficult to conceive of a sailor who would throw all else overboard. It is much easier to understand how he, like the Spanish, has conceded the vote to women by seeing them "less plagued by the liberalism that must be obliterated," according to a statement in a fascist newspaper. Women, it has been said, have never had the fetish of freedom, and they will agree that the only politics that matter to any country are economic politics. The vote of the "homemakers" will always be given to the party that governs by providing decent wages and a stable diet.

Even though I am not particularly inclined toward fascism, in all honesty I must celebrate the success of judiciousness and the cautious observance of political morality manifest in the feminist form of representation adopted in Spain. It has liberated María de Maeztu, Doña Blanca de los Ríos and their companions from the contemptible conflict of the polls with bombastic speeches in the plazas or in the mercenary search for votes. Only that in their case they have attempted to achieve with feminism an insignificant amount, of a rather noxious chemistry. One María de Maeztu represents substantially her constituency, but the desire for justice of an entity as vast as the teachers' union cannot be satisfied with just one deputy even though she may possess these qualities. I commend and celebrate this as an insinuation of the genuine order of the labor union, which has yet to come, for the organization of national activities both in Spain and in America.

The fact that Mr. Mussolini himself resurrects the unions' representation, even though it may be with the hand of the Left, actually works to our benefit and compels us to slowly and cautiously approach the absolute order that has been fully restored.

For the same reasons that these two political patrons have been able to grant the vote without a struggle—and, in Spain, I believe, even without the volition of women of the upper class—the French leftists have denied it. They fear this formidable party of "homemakers," this duplication of voters forged from an element neither Jacobean nor Communist. They think that, at most, some liberals from a less extreme, less militant liberalism would go to the polls to vote. The Communists have learned to be more rational and, in the face of risks, they voted in accordance with their programs.

What has occurred in Spain and Italy is of great importance for our America. It is possible that Mexico repeat the panic and the resolution of the

French Congress; it is highly likely that Uruguay will do something similar. As for the rest of the nations, however, it is fairly apparent that they will grant to us women the right to vote, with immense pressure, in defense of that hypothetical Communism which they so greatly fear.

It is, then, time for our feminists, for the fruit of my anti-feminist mystique, as unjustified as the feminist one they gave me in Cuba, from my point of view, out of the most pure and good intentions.

According to the dauntless feminists that have grilled me for having desired "a division of labor on the basis of gender," I am a woman from the Middle Ages that has never worked, that in her idleness creates aesthetic systems and betrays the female workers by writing against their most vital interests. According to another that I once met in a certain country, with my appalling discourse I would be an outstanding barricade leader. According to Mr. Marius André, upon my arrival in Paris this time, I was coming to incite the Communist masses against the clergy. All this was written in the noble French of Marius André and published in the *Revue de L'Amerique Latine*.

I do not believe, however, that support has been added to my feminist mystique. I have never written any praise of this political party, even though within it I cherish and esteem many of its female leaders. As for my anticlerical conferences in Santiago, Chile, that is a matter of the trusty information about us that the Europeans possess. My noble friend Ventura García Calderón took too seriously my defense in the French magazine and sacrificed for it the co-direction that she had there, which was far more valuable than a senseless rumor from overseas.

The feminine right to vote has always seemed to me an unquestionably natural thing. But, I distinguish between right and wisdom; and between "natural" and "sensible." There are rights that I am not interested in exercising since they would leave me as lowly as before. I do not believe in the parliament of women, just as I do not believe in that of men. When in that New Chile, which I encountered upon my return and in which I had the pleasure of not believing, they spoke of the new Constitution, even though I understood little or nothing about the proposition that two conventional schoolteachers made regarding unions, I warmly accepted it. Naturally, it was not a question of the official guilds of Mussolini, in which one half of the representatives are elected by the government and the other half by the official unions, rather something more closely resembling representation in medieval Florence, in which the guild or union not manipulated by official authorities could elect freely.

My friends' proposition was not even considered for two minutes. The pseudo-conventionalists, on the other hand, were not going to discuss but rather accept decisions already taken. In those days, and as they might have discussed the idea, presenting it as a Bolshevik creation, I said, in an informal talk for the Night School organized by the association of architects, the little that I knew of the organization of the unions in the Middle Ages. It is the only occasion in which I have allowed myself to articulate an opinion on electoral topics that are not mine, and that I did not seek to wrest from either the men or the feminists themselves.

Of a similar Parliament it would important for me to continue my works and even assist them in a gossip column, without attempting to end up as a female deputy, or even an advisor. I would gladly listen to a female delegate of the dressmakers, to that of the elementary schoolteachers, to each and every one of the cobblers or textile workers, to speak of theirs legitimately, presenting in living flesh that which is their livelihood. But I would guard against giving my time to an unemployed leader who represents the insubstantial, in much the same way a deputy with imprecise speech does not capture any definite concept or interest.

The confused corporation of today, in which nobody represents anybody, does not interest me in the least, even when one half of it is comprised of women. I am skeptical of any fundamental changes or renovations of the national entrails under the current regime, in which the farmer speaks about schools and the attorney passes judgment on the universe...

I ask to be forgiven for the personal references that surface in this article. I have made good use of it to reply to some insidiously candid remarks, and also to some insolent comments about my feminist phobia, which, for the past two years, I have not addressed, opting to remain in patient silence.

(Paris, May 1928)

NEW HORIZONS FAVOR WOMEN

A group of representatives has presented a simple legislative proposal of considerable importance to women, because it opens new horizons of work opportunities, and because it attempts to secure for them a more extensive field of action, in accordance with their intellectual capabilities and with their gender.

It concerns the granting of a considerable discount in the licenses of those stores whose personnel is at least seventy-five percent female. The discount that, in this resolution, might affect the municipalities where the measure would be implemented, will be compensated for with an increase in the taxes paid by the businesses of alcoholic beverages.

Nothing is more just, more logical, or more natural than this proposal. Let us dare to say that with its implementation, we are attempting to put an end to the veritable shame of the masculine sex.

Isn't it true that, in effect, the male clerks of fabric stores, who cut meters of ribbons, present themselves as experts in corsets and other genuinely feminine articles and at the same time are usurping positions, jobs, and occupations that rightfully pertain to women?

The press has often expressed concern with these anomalies; but as their well-intentioned admonitions have not brought results, it is righteous that what should have been done long ago for the sake of feminine dignity, is now being done through the proper legal channels.

The only thing one would have to request is that when these jobs are executed by women the employers pay the same salaries to them as to the men who once occupied these positions. Precisely because something curious happens with respect to this matter, something that constitutes a wicked injus-

167

tice: when a women occupies a position that was once held by a man, her salary subsequently decreases.

For what reason? Because women generally provide a sounder guarantee of sobriety, honesty, and consistent attendance? Why don't they declare strikes in the manner of the uglier sex? Quite simply, it just is not fair. The law would merely attempt to convey this feeling. Otherwise, the owners of stores would cheat the deserving and reward the undeserving.

With respect to men, it is important that they continue to exercise their energies, their strength, and their activities in ways other than selling skeins of silk and spools of thread.

(Punta Arenas, February 21, 1919)

AN OPINION ON FEMINISM

The entrance of women into the work force, a most significant contemporary event, should have brought about a change in the organization of labor
in society. This did not, in fact, happen, and instead a veritable barbarism was
created, about which I would like to say a word or two. Thus I will begin to
deliver my opinion on feminism, with the goal of alleviating myself of a pon-
derous weight.

What we regard as contemporary civilization, which attempts to realize a
work of material and intellectual order, a rearranged worldly discipline, up
until the present time has not even considered one of the most basic, fundamentally basic, principles: the organization of labor according to gender.

Women have made their entrance into the realm of every human occupation. According to the feminists, this is a triumphant moment, a vindication,
somewhat belated yet praiseworthy, of our capabilities, which, according to
them, parallel those of the man. For me, this is not the entrance of a Roman
conqueror; nor is there such universal success.

The brutal inhumanity of the factory has been opened for woman; the
repulsiveness of some jobs, which simply put are wretched, have incorporated
women into their labor unions. These totally heartless professions, essentially
the equivalence of disgusting exchange of labor for money, have welcomed
women into their slimy quagmire. Before celebrating the opening of these
doors, it was fundamental to have examined which doors were opening, and
before putting one's foot inside this new universe, one had to have looked
backwards toward that which was being abandoned to measure it with an
unhurried and thoughtful eye.

Woman is the first one to blame: she has wanted to be incorporated into any and everything, to be taken into account in every professional office where the owner was male and which, by being an inviolable domain for her, took on for her the appearance of a fairy tale palace. One cannot deny that her incorporation into each one of the masculine jobs has been swift; it is with vertigo that she rolls down the precipice. We already have the female doctor (blessed be that salary!), but opposite this we have the female chauffeur; opposite the children's attorney is the railway-worker (the one who cleans the rails); opposite the university professor is the explosives worker and the miserable door-to-door magazine saleswoman or the streetcar conductor. In other words, we have entered, at once, into both the eminent professions and the more detestable, less fortunate jobs.

It is entirely a symptom of these times that in the latest "International Feminist Congress," which took place in Paris, a woman (one of the most distinguished female representatives) articulated the proposition quoted by the French press as "all laws should be abolished, one by one, that, by conceding certain privileges to the working woman, create a situation of difference with respect to males." This proposition, with a preposterousness that surpasses all reasonable objectives, advocates the elimination of the professed "law of the chair," the elimination of maternity leave customarily granted to the female worker one month prior to and one month following childbirth, among other things. The proponent contended that, if the woman were to evade any responsibility expected of her male counterpart, at once she would diminish her right to vote and other legal privileges extended to males. The partisans of this proposition spoke about "mathematical justice," "pure logic," and other such absurdities.

Debates like this serve, within their gross offensiveness, to delineate camps, to profiles ideologies, and to clearly map out the dual nature—the crazed virgins and the prudent virgins—of these astonishing assemblies. There is a band of ultra-Amazons and daring Valkyries that demand with rashness (which arouses in me more pity than irritation) obligatory military service and the elimination of gender in the language. And there are some more reactionary or "conservative" feminists who believe that new legislation should be directed by physiological imperatives, which can be translated essentially into the following: woman will be equal to man when she has no breast for nursing and she does not carry within her body life-bearing capacities. In other words, someday on one of those other planets, which theosophers explore in their heavens.

170

Until today I have not believed in the celebrated intellectual equality of the sexes; I tend to regard myself as even below these "conservative" feminists, and thus I greatly hesitate to answer affirmatively for the umpteenth time to the question of the day: Are you a feminist? It almost seems more honest to flatly answer no: I lack the time to deliver a lengthy declaration of principles.

Nonetheless, it is beneficial to invent some sort of conservative program for feminism. I would place at the center of the program the following article: We request an organization of human labor that divides the tasks into three groups. Group A: Professions or jobs reserved exclusively for males on account of the greater physical strength or superior creativity required and which women cannot attain. Group B: Professions or jobs reserved exclusively for females, on account of their physical capabilities or due to their direct relationship with children. Group C: Professions or jobs that can be served equally well by men or women.

The first division maintains necessary contrasts: manual labor in the same category as the kind of work that could be viewed as world leadership. Here one would find everyone from the coal miner to Aristotle, the philosophical consultant and the popular politician.

The second would be directed so as to whisk away men from the frivolous activities in which he becomes effeminate, losing his manly dignity and appearing as an absolute intruder.

The final category would encompass numerous activities that are simply impossible to define as either masculine or feminine, given that they require a moderate expenditure of energy. These do not necessitate that a woman run the danger of exhausting herself, nor that a man make a living in a distasteful position.

I do not want a woman to be president of the Court of Justice, even though it is my impression that she is very well suited for Juvenile Court. The question of supreme justice is the most ideal of this world; it requires an absolute maturity of conscience, a panoramic vision of all human existence, which women rarely possess. (I would venture to say never have.) Nor do I desire that she be queen—in spite of the Isabellas—because almost always the government of a queen is essentially that of brilliant ministers.

And I experience a genuine nausea on account of those monstrous military exercises which are taking place in Russia, and which someone unknown to me is seeking to take to fascist Italy.

In spite of Joan of Arc, indeed, in spite of her efforts: the poor maiden of France marks with her actions a time in which man must have become utterly debased to ineffable limits. The most disgraceful thing that can happen to a woman in this world is to represent with her marvelous deeds the degradation of man, her natural guide, her natural defender, her natural hero.

It is essentially an appeal to desperate and fraudulent arguments to give the name of Madame Curie in order to immediately seek a national presidency. It is also naïve to request female popes because of the existence of Saint Teresa, who would have answered with a witty joke had they even suggested nominating her for a cardinalship.

The topic is significant and I intend to return to it in the future.

(July 1927)

GABRIELA MISTRAL: A CHRONOLOGICAL BIOGRAPHY

1889—Lucila Godoy Alcayaga was born in Vicuña, Chile, on April 7th to her parents, Jerónimo Godoy Villanueva and Petronila Alcayaga.

1904-1909—Teacher in the schools "La Compañía" and La Cantera, and Teacher's Assistant in La Serena.

1909—On November 25th Romelio Ureta commits suicide, the one for whom Lucila "professed a profound spiritual affection."

1911—Professor and Inspector of the Schools of Traiguén, Los Andes and Antofagasta.

1914—In the Floral Games (*Juegos Florales*) celebrated in Santiago, Chile, she obtains the highest distinction of honor—flowers, a gold medal and a crown of ivy—with "The Sonnets of Death." From this moment she began to use her literary pseudonym: Gabriela Mistral.

1918-1920—Professor and director of the schools in Punta Arenas (today, Magallanes), the southernmost city of Chile, and in Temuco.

1921—On May 14th, the Liceo #6 of Santiago, Chile is founded; Mistral is named director.

1922—At the invitation of Secretary of Public Education José Vasconcelos, she moves to Mexico with the purpose of collaborating in the country's momentous educational reforms and in the organization and establishment of public libraries.

Her first book, *Desolación*, appears in New York, edited by the Instituto de las Españas, under the direction of Federico de Onís.

1923—A statue of Mistral is erected in Mexico in a public park. She prepares the publication of *Readings for Women*, a selection of literary pages, to be used in the school that bears her name.

1924—First trip to United States and then to Europe (Italy, Spain, France, etc.). Her poems for children (songs, lullabies, rounds, etc.) are gathered in *Ternura*, which is edited in Madrid.

1925—Retirement in Chile as a schoolteacher, with the intention of settling indefinitely on her native soil.

1926—Attendance at the Assembly of the League of Nations as Chile's representative.

Travel to Río de la Plata and visits to Argentina and Uruguay.

Assumes the position of secretary of the Institute of Intellectual Cooperation in France.

1927-1928—Fulfills diplomatic missions to the Educational Congresses of

Locarno, the University Federations of Madrid, the Cinematographic Institute of Rome, etc.

1931—Extensive travels throughout Central America and the Antilles. Period of giving conferences and receiving honors.

1932—Beginning of her consular career, which she carries out successively in Italian, Spanish and Portuguese cities.

1935—Designated perpetual Consul of the Republic of Chile as a consequence of a law approved by the Chilean Congress under President Pedro Aguirre Cerda. From then on she travels and resides in European and American cities.

1938—Her second trip to Uruguay and Argentina. Her third book of poetry, *Tala*, is published by the journal, *Sur*, of Buenos Aires, under the direction of its editor, Victoria Ocampo. Profits from the sale of *Tala* were to go to Catalonian institutions, such as the Residencia de Pedralbes, which housed Basque children who were displaced because of the Spanish Civil War.
Triumphant return to Santiago de Chile.

1945—While in Brazil (Petrópolis) she receives news that she was awarded the Nobel Prize for Literature, the first Latin American writer to receive this honor, which she accepts in person from King Gustav of Sweden.

1951—Recipient of the Chilean National Prize for Literature.

1954—Publication of her last book of poetry, *Lagar*, as Volume VI of *Selected Works of Gabriela Mistral (Obras Selectas de Gabriela Mistral)*, in Santiago, Chile.
The next few years are spent in the North American town of Roslyn, New York.

1957—Mistral dies on January 10th in General Hospital of Hempstead, New York. The Chilean government decrees a three day period of national mourning; her body is returned to her "beloved town of Montegrande." By decree of her last will and testament, dated November 17, 1956, all proceeds from the sale of her books published in South America would benefit the impoverished children of Montegrande, Chile, a sparsely populated town which does not even appear on maps.

1958—Inauguration of the Gabriela Mistral High School in Puerto Rico. Publication of *Recados: Songs of Chile (Recados: Cantando a Chile)*, with prologue and notes by Alfonso M. Escudero, as Volume IV of *Selected Works of Gabriela Mistral (Obras Selectas de Gabriela Mistral)*, in Santiago, Chile.

The Editors

MARJORIE AGOSÍN

Marjorie Agosín, a native of Chile, has lived in exile in the United States for many years. She received her Ph.D. in Spanish-American Literature from Indiana University and is professor of Spanish at Wellesley College in Wellesley, Masachusetts. Well-known as a poet, writer, and human rights activist, she is a prolific author and a champion of women writers. She has served as editor for numerous volumes that brought Latin American women writers previously untranslated and largely unknown outside their homelands to the English-speaking audience.

Ms. Agosín is editor of the White Pine Press Secret Weavers Series: Writing by Latin American Women, of which this book is volume fifteen. This critically-acclaimed series was among the first series published in the United States specifically dedicated to the writing of Latin American women.

Marjorie Agosín's published works include *A Cross and A Star: Memoirs of a Jewish Girl in Chile, Ashes of Revolt,* both non-fiction; *Happiness,* a collection of stories; and *An Absence of Shadows,* poetry.

JACQELINE C. NANFITO

Jacqueline Nanfito is an associate professor of Spanish and Comparative Literature in the Department of Modern Languages and Literatures at Case Western Reserve University, in Cleveland, Ohio. The focus of her scholarly writing has been women writers of Latin America. She has written a book on the work of Sor Juana Inés de la Cruz (*El sueño: Cartographies of Knowledge and the Self),* which was published in the Peter Lang series Wor(l)ds of Change: Latin American and Iberian Literature.

Since coming to CWRU, she has been actively involved in promoting activities related to women, from teaching courses on Latin American women writers, to serving on the Women's Studies Program steering committee, the Women's Faculty Association steering committee, and as co-chair of the University Women's Coalition. In the fall of 1997, with the support of the Flora Stone Mather Alumnae Association, she organized an exhibition of *arpilleras,* the tapestries stitched by Chilean women in protest of the dictatorial regime of Augusto Pinochet, and helped choreograph a modern dance version of the *cueca sola,* which was performed at the opening reception of the exhibit.

Notes on the Work

For the *recados* we have used the following editions: *Recados para America: Textos de Gabriela Mistral*, Editorial Espesa, Santiago, Chile, 1978. Other *recados* were obtained from the book by Roque Esteban Scarpa, *Gabriela piensa en...* Editorial Andrés Bello, Santiago, Chile, 1978.

For a detailed biographic analysis of Gabriela Mistral, I suggest Elizabeth Horan, *Gabriela Mistral: An Artist and Her People*, Inter-American Cultural Series, published under the auspices of the Organization of American States. Also, I recommend the book by Jaime Concha, *Gabriela Mistral*, Madrid, Tauro, 1983 and the book by Marielise Gazarian Gautier, *Gabriela Mistral: The Teacher from the Valley of Elqui*, Chicago Franciscan Herald Press, 1975.

GABRIELA MISTRAL

1. "La maestra rural," *Desolación*, Edición de Jaime Quezada in *Gabriela Mistral: Poesía y prosa*. Edición de La Biblioteca Ayacucho, Caracas, Venezuela, 1993, p. 74.

2. Ibid, p. 75.

3. Included in *Desolación*.

4. Josefina Ludmer, "Las tretas del débil" in *La sartén por el mango*, Puerto Rico, Ediciones Huracán, 1987.

5. One of the most illuminating essays about Gabriela Mistral is the one by Adriana Valdés in *Composición de lugar: escritos sobre cultura*, Editorial Universo, Santiago, Chile, 1995. The article is titled "Gabriela Mistral: identidades tras la fuga. Lectura de Tala," pp. 196-214.

6. Gabriela Mistral, *Tala*, "La fuga," Edición Quezada, p. 113.

7. Could be roughly translated to "womanness."

8. *Tala*, "País de la ausencia," p. 152.

9. Many of these ideas about Mistral and her relation to Chilean politics and history come from statements made by Elizabeth Horan, especially in "Gabriela Mistral: Language is the Only Homeland" in *A Dream of Light and Shadow*, University of New Mexico Press, 1995 as well as an article entitled "Santa maestra muerta: Body and Nation in Portraits of Gabriela Mistral," *Taller de Letras*, Universidad Católica de Chile, 1998.

10. *Ternura*, p. 43.

MEMORY, RESISTENCE AND IDENTITY

1. "Correspondencia de Madrid; Recados: quiero ser noticiero de los míos, Impetu de comunicación, y brevedad," *Puerto Rico Ilustrado*, July 23, 1934. In Luis de Arrigoitía, *Pensamiento y forma en la prosa de Gabriela Mistral* (Río Piedras, P.R.: Editorial de la Universidad de Puerto Rico, 1989), p. 285. To date, Arrigoitía's text is the most comprehensive, authoritative historical/critical study of Mistral's prose.

2. Luis de Arrigoitía, *Pensamiento y forma en la prosa de Gabriela Mistral* (Río Piedras, P.R.: Editorial de la Universidad de Puerto Rico, 1989), p. 285.

3. Lydia Fakundiny, ed., *The Art of the Essay* (Boston: Houghton Mifflin, 1991), p 4.

4. Carmelo Virgillo, "Feminine Symbolism in Gabriela Mistral's "Fruta" in *Latin American Women Writers: Yesterday and Today* (Pittsburgh: Latin American Literary Review Press, 1977) pp. 105-114.

5. Amy Kaminsky, "Essay, Gender and Mestizaje" in *The Politics of the Essay*, eds. Ruth Ellen Boetcher Joeres and Elizabeth Mittman, (Bloomington: University of Indiana Press, 1993), p. 118.

6. Ruth-Ellen Boetcher Joeres and Elizabeth Mittman, eds. "[An] Introductory Essay" in *The Politics of the Essay*, p. 13.

7. "Sobre la mujer chilena" in *Política y espíritu* (Santiago de Chile, June 13, 1946); reprinted in *Gabriela Mistral, escritos políticos*. Selection, prologue and notes by Jaime Quezada, 2nd ed. (Mexico, Fondo de Cultura Económica: Colección Tierra Firme, 1995), pp. 62-63.

8. Introduction to Part 1 ("Women, Self, Writing") of *Women's Writing in Latin America: An Anthology*, eds. Sara Castro-Klarén, Sylvia Molloy and Beatriz Sarlo (Boulder Westview Press, 1991), p. 14.

9. "Viajar" (June, 1927) in *Gabriela anda por el mundo*, selection of prose and prologue by Roque Estéban Scarpa (Santiago, Chile: Andrés Bello, 1978, p. 20.

10. "Mensaje sobre Luisa Luisi" (February, 1941), p. 67.

11. "Cómo escribo" (January, 1938), in Gabriela Mistral: *Paginas en prosa*, Ed. María Hortensia Lacaui. Selection, prologue and notes by José Pereira Rodríguez (Buenos Aires: Editorial Kapelusz, 1962), p. 3.